# Information Technology
# and the Individual

# Information Technology and the Individual

*Edited by Jack Meadows*

Pinter Publishers
London and New York

First published in Great Britain in 1991 by
Pinter Publishers Limited
25 Floral Street, London WC2E 9DS

**British Library Cataloguing in Publication Data**

A CIP catalogue record for this book is available from the
British Library
ISBN 0 86187 877 9


For enquiries in North America, please contact
PO Box 197, Irvington, NY10533

**Library of Congress Cataloging-in-Publication Data**

Information technology and the individual / edited by Jack Meadows.
    p.  cm.
  Includes bibliographical references and index.
  ISBN 0-86187-877-9.
  1. Information technology.    I. Meadows, A. J. (Arthur Jack)
HC79.I55I539 1991
303.4'833--dc20                                                    90-27685
                                                                        CIP


Typeset by Witwell Limited, Southport
Printed and bound in Great Britain by Biddles Ltd of Guildford and
Kings Lynn

# Contents

# List of contributors

**Douglas Badenoch** is a lecturer in the Department of Information Science at the University of Strathclyde. Teaching and research interests include information retrieval, user modelling and natural language processing. He maintains involvement with an Esprit project applying NLP to the automatic indexing and classification of technical documentation.

**Patricia Baird** has been a senior lecturer in the Department of Information Science at the University of Strathclyde, where her main areas of teaching and research were in electronic publishing, optical disc technologies and hypertext. Director of several hypertext research projects – including the *Glasgow Online* system – and editor of *Hypermedia*, an international journal on hypertext and related areas published by Taylor Graham. Since January 1991, she has been Information Services Manager at the *Daily Record* newspaper.

**Blaise Cronin** is currently Dean and Professor, School of Library & Information Science, Indiana University. From 1985-1991 he was Professor of Information Science and Head of the Department of Information Science, University of Strathclyde. He is the author/editor of more than 150 books, reports and articles and is fellow of the Institute of Information Scientists, the Library Association and the British Institute of Management.

**Elisabeth Davenport** holds degrees in Greek and English Literature, Information Science, and is completing a degree in Biological and Earth Sciences with the Open University. She is currently a lecturer in the Department of Information Science at Strathclyde, where her main teaching and research areas are information management, the creation of knowledge and the legal status of electronic text.

**R. J. Hartley** lectures in information retrieval and information science in the Department of Information & Library Studies, University College of Wales, Aberystwyth. He is joint author of *Online searching: principles and practice* (Bowker-Saur, 1990) and joint editor of *Online information retrieval today and tomorrow* (Learned Information, 1990). He is currently Treasurer of the UK Online User Group. He has written numerous papers on aspects of information retrieval and library applications of information technology.

**Noreen MacMorrow** is a lecturer in the Department of Information Science at the University of Strathclyde. Her main areas of teaching and research are database management systems, hypermedia and information policy. Research projects include co-directing a number of hypertext projects within the department, and, in conjunction with Solon Consultants (London), implementation of a full-text database of European Parliament documents and information service provision for DECTA (the Developing Countries Trade Agency). She is an associate editor of *Hypermedia* and the author of several papers on hypertext and hypermedia.

**Anne Martin** worked on this project while on the MA Information Studies course at Sheffield University in 1987–8. Since then she has been in Glasgow, first as Information Manager for the HCI (Human Computer Interaction) Library and Information Service based at the Turing Institute, and since December 1990 as Information Manager for Hall Aitken Associates, a European Research Information and Consultancy firm. She is a member of the Institute of Information Scientists.

**Jack Meadows** is currently Professor of Library and Information Studies at Loughborough University. Formerly Head of the Departments of Astronomy and History of Science and of the Primary Communications Research Centre at Leicester University.

**Howard Petrie** is a Principal Administrator for information systems development in the Directorate General for substantive examination in the European Patent Office in Munich. He has previously held posts at the Commission of the European Communities, at various universities and in research.

**Bob Usherwood** is a Senior Lecturer in the Department of Information Studies, University of Sheffield. Prior to joining the university, he was Chief Librarian in the London Borough of Lambeth. He has lectured widely in this country and overseas and is the author of numerous publications including two books, *The Visible Library* and *The Public Library as Public Knowledge*.

**John Williams** is Senior Lecturer, Department of Law, University College of Wales, Aberystwyth, where he lectures in Family Law and International Law. He is author of *Social Services Law* (Fourmat Publishing, 1988) and *The Law of Mental Health* (Fourmat, 1990). He is the author of many articles on family law, social services law and international law.

# Preface

One of the more notable statistics in the world of information is the good correlation between the number of computers in existence and the global production of paper. A significant part of that increase in paper consumption must be due to the amount written about information technology and its prospects. So what is the justification for another title?

In the first place, our interest is in the 'information' part of 'information technology'. The technology component is mentioned only to the extent that its development affects the communication of information. More particularly, we are concerned here with information that is generated by organisations, but is aimed at individuals, and is required by the latter if they are to function happily and efficiently in society. Institutions which generate such information are to be found, for example, in the mass media, law, education, banking and the retail trade. The question we shall be examining is not only how new technology will affect the process of acquisition of information from these bodies, and interaction with them, but also how it will alter the form and content of the information made available.

The authors have a rather different background from that of many writers on information technology. Our training in information work has led us to a particular concern with the information needs of the end-user and in how these needs might best be met. Our contributions to this book therefore concentrate on the information activities of the individual at a time when satisfaction of his, or her, requirements is in a state of flux due to the rapidity of technological change. It is far from easy to see, as yet, whether the net effect will be beneficial for the individual, or not. Information technology can certainly centralise control over information — for example, by bringing together information about an individual that has previously been distributed over a number of separate outlets. But, equally, it can act to decentralise control: the power and flexibility of the information retrieving and handling devices available to individuals is greater now than at any time in history.

In a sense, the origins of this book reflect this new power and flexibility. An experimental network was established in the latter part of the 1980s between some of the library and information studies departments in the UK to see what the pros and cons of electronic interchange between them might be. It was found that a number of people in these departments were concerned with research into the impact of information technology on the individual. It was therefore decided to communicate on this topic via the network, which was consequently labelled PILNET (the personal information for living network). The present book grew out of this initiative.

We are happy to acknowledge with gratitude here the grant from the British Library Research and Development Department which allowed this experiment to be undertaken. It should be emphasised that their provision related only to the running of the project. The content of communications via PILNET, as reflected in this book, can be blamed only on the editor and the contributors.

# CHAPTER 1

# From tuple to text: some thoughts on personal data in the UK

*Elisabeth Davenport and Blaise Cronin*

## Introduction

Mass storage of personal data presents obvious, and often rehearsed problems, in terms of data integrity and data security; breaches, intentional and non-intentional, occur in both areas. These are the areas tackled in law (both case law and legislation), and may be labelled as exogenous or extrinsic problems, as they depend on human input or interference.

The law does not yet recognise the aggregation, manipulation and interpretation of personal data as an area of potential personal damage, though recent European concern may result in modification of national legislations (DG XIII, 1990, p. 1). Such secondary processes may be called intrinsic or systemic features of data handling and they are enabled and encouraged by the development of integrative networks and software attached to major systems (the STATUS package used by the Police National Computer (PNC), for example); they will be further enhanced by emergent interactive multimedia technologies (Campbell, 1986, pp. 46ff.; Jones, 1988, pp. 32 ff.).

Aggregation and manipulation are the *raisons d'être* of systems which have moved beyond their primary function as transaction processors; they sustain the vitality of the data held, as it can be reconfigured, restructured and faceted into fresh subject material. Tuples,* or the elements of records, are no longer treated as definitive statements of details collected for a specific and stated purpose, but become elements in what Zuboff has described as 'an enormous, dynamic, fluid, electronic text' which allows unknown readers to interact with personal data in unknown ways, or, in other words, to write scripts or texts round personal data over which data subjects have no control (Marx, 1990, pp. 12 ff).

The public as a whole is naïve about secondary processing, and recent figures from the Data Registrar confirm the obsession with financial and health data as primary areas of concern. The Registrar, himself, would like to raise awareness of secondary processing, but his means are limited. Though the law may not recognise secondary processing as a problem area, there is public disquiet about 'the uses to which data are put' (this issue is as high in the scale of public concern as right of access and accuracy, the 'openness' and 'the right to correct' covered by the Data Protection Act) where the focus is on re-sale, or re-setting (passing on of mailing lists, for example), rather than manipulation.

The Registrar suggests that fuller information on secondary uses may not solve the problem for three reasons:

1. it is clear that most people do not read or understand 'small print' on application forms or questionnaires. They tend to form a view about what the information will be used for from the context of the transaction or from the parts of a form that they are actually completing.
2. the full meaning of an explanation will often not be apparent, because of general ignorance of the data handling practices and technical possibilities.
3. even if it were possible to make people fully aware of what might happen, the pressures on them to give the information (because they want or need the loan, the house or the goods, or because it is required by law) are likely to outweigh any reservations they may have about the secondary uses. (Data Protection Registrar, 1989, p. 4320/21).

---

*An n-tuple is a representation of some idea, entity, or concept which uses n attributes. For example, a tuple used to describe personnel records in a relational database might have three — name, expertise and department.

Distinctions which might be valid in a formal analysis of personal data usage — was the information supplied on a voluntary or involuntary basis? will it remain attached to an individual or will it be aggregated and interpreted in terms of a group identity? should policy be framed in terms of the demand (the data user) or supply (the data subject) side? — are of little interest to many data subjects, who are unaware of statistical methodologies, and often passive in their response to government demands. Public concern is activated on a large scale only by specific societal issues, like the Poll Tax, the disclosure of AIDS information, registration of football fans, some of which we discuss below.

## The background

This chapter reflects our interest in the uses and abuses of publicly held personal data. Three years ago, when PILNET was proposed, the Data Protection Act was in the early stages of its implementation. Though the effectiveness of the Act as an instrument of protection has been questioned, and though it has been widely demeaned as a minimalist and pragmatic response to European demands for conforming legislation (Birkinshaw, 1987), it has concentrated attention on digitised data as an information form with novel and unforeseeable effects. The Office of the Data Registrar has emerged as an intelligent and active department whose monitoring of the evolution of protection under the Act (published in the annual reports of the Registrar) is a ready resource for researchers.

Like other informatics legislation in the UK (such as the Copyright, Designs and Patents Act 1988), the Data Protection Act appears both myopic and astigmatic; this is partly due to the fact that it has been framed in terms which must be defined in case law. By focusing on 'holdings' and the accuracy and access problems which attach to these, it avoids the issues of secondary processing, particularly networking (presumably covered by other legislation, like the catch-all Interception of Telecommunications Act (Jones, 1986, pp. 14–16)). The Registrar, however, has been vigilant in his raising of issues as technological practice evolves, and secondary processing is a major area of concern in his most recent report. Much of what we say in this chapter has emerged from our

reading of these reports, but we, as academics, go beyond the
Registrar and anticipate the impact of emergent technologies.
We focus on four areas where personal information in electronic form is networked (we take a broad view of the term and
take it as equivalent to 'shared' or 'put into contact with',
which may, or may not mean physical cabling):

1. the individual as citizen (government data);
2. as colleague (data attached to the workplace);
3. as consumer (of goods and services); and
4. as companion (data related to the pursuit of leisure).

Many of the contributors to the PILNET project have
emphasised the beneficial potential for augmentation offered
by networked personal information (their definition of the
term might be 'information which satisfies an individual or
personal inquiry' and this is the perspective of the chapters on
health information and community information, topics which
we do not discuss as they are covered elsewhere). Our interest
is the downside, the technical, ethical and above all political
implications of public holdings (local and central government, company or club) of personal data on individuals, and
the construction, through processing and linking and networking, of externally defined profiles or legal personae,
linked more or less tenuously (through an ID, a name or an
address) to a physical person.

In the context of such legal, official or commercial purposes,
personal information means 'information which relates to a
living individual who can be identified from that information
(or from that and other information in the possession of the
authority keeping the record) including any expression of
opinion about the individual but not any indication of the
intentions of the authority with respect to that individual'
(Scottish Current Law Statutes, 1987, c. 37).

By approaching the public use of personal data from the
perspective of different roles in an individual life (rather than
primarily by administrative or industrial sector, 'personal
information in the health service', or 'personal information in
education' or 'personal information in the mail order business'), we hope to redress the balance of discussion in favour
of the data subject; current legislation and policies have
focused on data users, or those who hold information on
others.

We have supplemented the material from the Data Registrar with a range of material — press cuttings, monographs, reports. Coverage is patchy as this is not an area where fundamental and lasting structures can be easily observed: the dance or interchange of public perceptions, new technology, and data user interests is free-form and volatile, and personal data issues are often publicised as part of larger political campaigns. Many of the published texts on the Government Data Network (GDN) are minimalist in their reporting of details; the one monograph which does probe its implications is the work of a prominent opposition journalist, Duncan Campbell (1986). Central government's campaign to 'democratise' certain local government services (notably health and education) by opening files to the public has raised new problems for personal data. Though bi-directional access to personal information is an established work practice in many organisations (through the appraisal interview, for example), just how acceptable to employees is the release of performance information to those outside the organisation?

## The issues

Certain crucial questions demand attention:

1. how pervasive is secondary processing and what are its effects on policy?
2. how much leakage is there between datasets within each of our four contexts?
3. how much leakage is there across the four contexts?
4. what are the main areas of public concern?
5. is a public awareness campaign necessary?

## Government data: the cabinet of Doctor Caligari

In 1986, Duncan Campbell mapped the extent and the history to date of government data holding in the UK. His research was published in the book we alluded to above, and contributed to a series of television programmes which became a *cause célèbre*, as tapes were confiscated and subjected to official interdict. The incident was considered by some as an apt illustration of the official UK approach to the two major issues of freedom of information and protection of privacy.

Campbell addressed the subject of what he called 'scaling' and 'linking' (the aggregation, manipulation and interpretation that are systemic features of mass processing), and mentioned plans for a comprehensive and integrated government data network (the GDN) envisaged for the 1990s. The system was put out to tender and a contract awarded to a private consortium, which has given adequate assurance on security (Preston, 1988).

Security, in terms of control of the uses to which data are put, will neither be required, nor embedded in the system; such constraint would dilute the system's potential as a tool for the profiling and integrating of individual datasets. The Data Protection Act is limited to empowering 'openness' and 'the right to correct'. The Data Registrar has offered assistance and advice to the Director of the Central Computing and Telecommunications Agency (CCTA) on security implications:

> It is in the use of the network that the key issues lie . . . I have been pleased by statements that Government Departments impose their own strict rules on disclosures of personal data from one to another. I believe it would be valuable if these rules were published. (Data Protection Registrar, 1987, Section 4.189[1]).

The information handled by the four initial departments of the GDN (Health and Social Security, Customs and Excise, Inland Revenue and the Home Office) covers categories of personal information which the public considers sensitive: tax, salaries, health and details of criminal convictions. It is not clear when the system will be fully integrated and running, as systems in the four member departments are at different stages of development. Some services (DHSS) are more completely computerised than others. The Inland Revenue in Scotland is computerised, but not in the whole of England; the extent of computerisation of police records varies from region to region (Campbell, 1986, pp. 62-7, 98, 115). Extension of the network is likely, as open systems protocols are adopted and data capture is standardised. Some departments (Driving Vehicle Licensing Centre (DVLC), Office of Population Censuses and Surveys (OPCS)) already feed into departments on the network; other registers (the Community Charge) are likely to be based on information from the networked departments (Data Protection Registrar, 1987, Section 4. 186).

Two areas which must be addressed are the use of aggregated data for inference and control in the broadest sense, and government resale of tailored datasets. The interpretation of personal data to profile individuals in terms of key characteristics is established police practice; these characteristics are used to group individuals into classes, which can be used to identify individuals who can be linked to certain types of criminality:

> Because most crime is random and opportunist, containment methods are based on selecting a population that is likely to commit random crime . . . Any member of the selected population is suspected not because reasonable grounds for suspicion exist, but because the person is a member of that population. (Pounder, 1986, p. 15)

The practice has led to occasional misidentification and misarrest. The quality of the data held in individual dossiers is questionable, as some authorities require records compiled from gossip, heresay and neighbourly observation (police are advised in Lothian to 'cultivate shopkeepers, tradesmen and garage proprietors who are good sources of information'), and performance is judged on the amount of information that individual officers feed to the records of local crime intelligence. Much of this trivia may be readily passed on by informers who are unaware that it appears on official electronic files.

Such profiling and targeting are common in market research, where the individual complies with the data-gathering exercise, and is under no obligation to purchase any products which emerge from the research exercise. Screening and targeting are not undesirable *per se*, and are essential in certain areas where personal information is in the hands of government, medical screening, for example, screening of children with special educational needs, or screening for eligibility for DHSS awards (an early application area for expert systems) (Portman, 1988). The Data Registrar expresses concern in his latest report that this practice should not be extended (Data Protection Registrar, 1989). The criteria of what is acceptable are context-dependent, a principle recognised by the Council of Europe, who have derived a framework of data protection rules based on the principle that 'specific sectors should be regulated by specific instruments' (DG XIII, 1990, p. 1).

The ethics of unforeseen aggregation and interpretation have been discussed in the context of commercial exploitation of government data, particularly of statistical, electoral and census data (Davenport and Cronin, 1987, pp. 8–12). Initial moves in this area emerged from the Rayner reports on efficiency across a range of government departments in the early 1980s. Government policy has moved beyond cost-recovery and now advocates income generation (guidelines were published by the Department of Trade and Industry) (Department of Trade and Industry, 1986). The guidelines are not contentious in themselves as they simply catch up with *de facto* exploitation of public data; but the extension of commercial exploitation to personal data may in some cases infringe rights of privacy.

If parts of the health service, for example, are privatised, does a commercial operator have the right to patient records for marketing purposes? Might he, or she, use such data to attract suppliers? What is the commercial status of police records, if parts of the prison service are privatised? If library services are contracted out, will membership and circulation files be the basis of quality-of-life analysis or market research for commercial products or service?

What should be the individual citizen's policy towards such exploitation of personal data? Should counter-measures be deployed, in terms of extension of the Data Protection Act? Should lobbies be established to insist that the data protection implications of any transfer of government responsibility to private hands are publicised and debated? Or should citizens welcome the personal profile as something which they themselves can exploit? A third-party entrepreneur might make an individual's datasets available in smart card format, which the citizen could match against profiles to his, or her, own advantage. A smart identity card, for example, might serve as a mediator between the individual and official information (a kind of virtual social worker), and allow him, or her, to establish what his(her) rights are on a specific issue; an ingenious implementation of such system allows peanut farmers in Georgia to check their subsidies, and the benefits of such a card have led to its introduction in a medical practice in Devon. In his Fifth Report, the Data Registrar considered a system in place in Essex in detail, where the card itself is the means of sorting and manipulating an individual's data (who decides what will be accessed, where and when), thus vesting control in the data subject rather than in an alien system. Such cards have featured in recent proposals to curb football hooliganism and under-age drinking (Data Protection Registrar, 1989, p. 4320/10).

Focused smart cards may be acceptable, but general purpose national ID cards are unlikely to be introduced in the UK, for cosmetic rather than libertarian reasons. The GDN already allows government to make the connections it requires (using national insurance, or whatever, as the link); to allow users access to a single password is to expose the operation to possible breaches of security. Data subjects have recently resisted the introduction of national ID cards in Australia (the government case was defeated on a technicality) and Canada, for more straightforward reasons of civil liberty (Brown, 1987; Greenleaf, 1988). The Data Registrar rather naïvely takes comfort in the discrepancy of formats, systems and files which exists across government data, as this will inhibit the emergence of the totalitarian record. Anyone who monitors the development of GOSIP (the government open systems information protocol), and the development of connectivity at every level of government information systems, must be more sceptical (Bartholomew, 1989; Judge, 1989).

## Poll Tax

The ethics of cross-fertilisation of government data is one of the issues raised by the introduction of the Community Charge, as attempts have been made to trace non-registrees and non-payers through a range of official files, at both local (library, housing records, the electoral register) and national (census) levels. Such extension of personal data contradicts the second principle of the Data Protection Act, which indicates that subjects must know why the information has been collected and how it will be used; the Registrar has expressed his disquiet in the Fifth Report, though this is likely to be one of many areas where he and government departments must beg to disagree.

To answer the questions raised as major issues in the context of this albeit brief resumé of government data handling:

1. yes — there is secondary processing, and yes, it impacts on policy, though it is difficult to gather evidence, and cases are only likely to come to light as scandals, or cases of maladministration.
2. yes — there is leakage across departments within the context of government data.
3. yes — there is leakage across our four contexts; government departments are actively encouraged to sell their data to external agencies.
4. yes — there is public concern, notably in the areas of tax and health data.
5. yes — public awareness should be increased, through civic education and so on; participative democracy depends on it. But, as the Registrar points out, the shibboleth of national security may inhibit this process.

## Employment data: poachers and gamekeepers

We have explored some of the consequences of aggregation and interpretation for personal information held by government agencies. These features of mass storage demand attention in the industrial and commercial context, where developments in integrative networking and distributed processing have produced a shift in approach for employer/employee relations from the personnel approach to human resource management.

Data handled by personnel departments have traditionally been derived from the taboo areas of health and remuneration, and have consequently been treated with discretion. The latter featured in the earliest applications of computer processing (payroll applications), and salary details have traditionally been kept separate from details of quality of performance (obviously they are related to number of hours worked), or domestic situation, which have been held on manual systems or relayed by word of mouth. This separation by media has prevented the aggregation, interpretation and profiling which are a feature of integrated information management systems.

In large organisations which feature associative or integrated information management systems, full compliance with the Data Protection Act may require a systems audit, or organisational data census, to establish patterns of ownership, use and access. In some case, such an audit may disrupt the political configuration of the organisation, as it may reveal principalities and states within the state. A Data Protection Audit might be used by a centralised data-processing manager to reassert authority over distributed subsystems, and rather than comply with the Act, some employers and departments may prefer to block access. An influential set of guidelines for employers, published by the National Computer Council, describes some techniques for evasion (registering data on manual files, or across multiple files, or keeping a hidden file). So much for the Registrar's confidence that professional guidelines will provide adequate safeguards.

Human resource management, however, demands integration and profiling for the optimal utilisation of manpower, and for projections of future deployment. Domestic details, details of health, past performance and skills training can be interpreted and matched against a typology to ensure best fit of resource and task. The technological base for computerised resource management is growing; between 1982 and 1988 there was a fourfold growth for the use of minicomputers in personnel, and a percentage increase in the use of micros from 4 per cent to 33 per cent.

The benefits of such profiling and targeting need not be confined to the demand, or data user, side. Employees can use such techniques to identify opportunities within the organisation, both professional and personal; they can also enhance their exploration of opportunities outside the company, the basis of the head-hunting databases which feed the employment market for sectoral specialists: 'career development and staff training are becoming precisely structured and goal-oriented activities' (Frenchman, 1988).

An extension of such services to the pre-employment market is offered by the Training Access Points (TAPs), which have been developed by the MSC/Training Commission; similar shop windows are offered on Prestel, where personal details

and proclivities can be matched with job and course des-
criptors. Such tailored information has been available for
some time through careers advisory services in parts of the
UK (prototypes were developed in the late sixties); many of
them emerged from batch processing systems, and distributed
PC processing has allowed their full potential to be realised. A
pan-European hypertext product offering ambient information, as well as details of training, is being produced in the
Department of Information Science at Strathclyde (Baird,
Cronin and Davenport, 1989).

A recent case study in the *Harvard Business Review* depicts
a totally informatised company, where technology is used for
surveillance (in the kindest sense) and harmonisation
(between work-force and task). Two of the ripostes which
accompany the case study decry the paternalism in this
scenario, which gives little indication of the potential for
increased employee responsibility, personal augmentation
and accountability (Marx, 1990). Such views are not, of
course, visionary. Many companies use networks and bulletin
boards as conceptual kasbahs for employees; managers pick
up novel projects and products from DEC's internal network,
as well as through more formal R & D processes. Open,
textualised systems like this allow personal information of a
different kind to be harvested; they allow colleagues to see
what lies behind the reductionist formats required by
structured databases (name, address and date of birth are
generally to be held to be an adequate distinguishing triplet
for most individuals), and get a feel for the individuals
involved. Personal testimony is, of course, a feature of existing personnel management, though it tends to appear in
fragmentary forms — like the appraisal transcript, the reference for a job, or the customer complaint — and is of little
value as an indicator of what it is like to work alongside a
named individual.

One technology which may offer a surrogate for this type of
experience is hypertext, which allows an individual's interaction with material (the texts, videos and recordings which
represent a particular workspace) to be tracked and analysed,
and can provide intimate insight into a colleague's understanding and feeling for problems and issues. The workspace,
for example, might be the fitting room of an auto-manu-
facturer, like Peugeot, who have combined video, voice-over

and text to produce computer-based training (CBT) for apprentices. The company responsible for such material, Hyperdoc, claims that more than 60 per cent of UK commercial sales of their product are for CBT applications.

Training might help apprentices to navigate through the overt procedures which are embodied in rule books and manuals. Such applications may extend beyond the engineering domain to public administration: hypertext is already being used to facilitate and accelerate the processing of DHSS claims in the UK and other countries (British Library, 1989).

But can technology help with the *social* constructs of office life? Let us assume that you have passed appropriate examinations, vetted by the appropriate professional body (these will probably have taught you to use the rule book), and you are now on the threshold of your first large department. How long will it take to find out where the pattern of reporting depicted in your training material diverges from the actual power base? With an integrated information base, which allows you to follow the links between memos, correspondence, inventories, bulletin boards and e-mail, you may be able to pick up the correct cues more quickly, and insert your own comments and observations. Decisions, designs, reports (and other such products of meetings) can be scrutinised; key or controversial points can be traced back through previous versions to their origins, in a process which may be described as 'decisional archaeology'.

Apprenticeship might involve a 'back-to-the-future' scenario, where the trainee reworks a critical decision, using departmental archives, by forward movement from historical input into group reports by individual members of cabals, cabinets, working parties and sub-committees, assessing the impact of their contributions. Success can be acknowledged, and failure used positively, as anatomised mistakes become learning tools. The apprentice can learn quickly what and what not to say, when and when not to say it, and whom to pass it on to. By handling 'problems having to do with reference and the nature of the relationships between one text and another', a trainee can acquire appropriate powers of judgment (Slatin, 1988).

Such a process of getting under the skin of colleagues is a new type of personal information gathering, and one which has hitherto not been formally managed, let alone subject to regulation under Data Protection. But it may become an important personnel resource, as company turnovers accelerate. Multiple apprenticeships may be a fact of life, where employees are continuously redeployed. Formal descriptions may be less important than individual style in attuning newcomers; and shadowing, and mentoring, with appropriate technology platforms, may be as important a part of apprenticeship as technical skills. Learning the ropes in such an environment may entail attaché or adjutant-type duties.

Apprentices must make their own sense of what they do in the organisation, and should be encouraged, within reason, to script themselves, trying out moves with other colleagues. A hypertext which offers simple and unified access to as wide a range of information as is feasible (total intelligence) can support such play. Apprentices may wish to monitor the ripple effects of sales gossip about new competitor products — has news of what rivals are up to produced a new venture in the R & D department? Did a specific tip from financial analysts on a competitor's quarterly returns allow a salesman to clinch a deal? Such information implies sharing of details of personal performance, or personal achievement, which can only be effective where employees agree not to insist on privacy in the interests of collegiality.

Social skills of the conventional sort must be acquired wherever relocation transforms an experienced employee into an apprentice. This may happen where there are internal moves in the organisation, or the company enters joint ventures with outsiders, or operates across national boundaries, wherever a rapid process of acculturation is required (by allowing comfortable access to anything from the etiquette of the open door, or appropriate body language, to the political and economic institutions of a host country). Such observation of the social behaviour of recognisable individuals, like shadowing their use of texts, implies exploitation of personal information, but personal information which is defined in terms that almost preclude protection under the Act.

These will, of course, be supplemented by social skills of the sort we have already described, grasping how, why and when things are done. What are the roles, rules, risks and rewards which define the new working environment? What counts as an issue for that department, which of these are priorities, how are they best resolved? One approach is to use real-time

negotiation as a learning experience; another is to plunder the
archives for something that looks similar, and work out how
that was handled. The business archive as a treasury of
strategies (using the past to make sense of the future) has
come into its own.

We are emphasising the emergent, qualitative, technology-
supported approach to getting to know one's colleagues
because it has been largely unexplored as an area of personal
information management in the workplace, though it has
major implications in terms of personal space. How happy
will employees be to have their past performance anatomised
and exploited? Let us take the case of a trainee salesman for a
large computing manufacturer, who may be new to the company, or may have been transferred from one account to
another. What does he, or she, need to acquire? A variegated
mass of social intelligence; some of it will already be available
as standard sales data, like names, personal details, product
details, order backlogs, projected delivery dates, audits of
previous purchases; but much of it (the vital detail which lies
behind the standard record) will be trapped inside his pre-
decessor's, or a rival salesman's head, though manifest in the
deals achieved, which makes archives (what has happened
when colleagues have been faced with similar problems in
other companies in this sector) invaluable.

Apprenticeship for salesmen is in transition. In the past it
has been of the traditional sort — shadowing, osmosis,
observing physical cues to assess the degree of client interest,
spotting when the moment is ripe for clinching a deal, picking
up tips from colleagues (often by phone). But where salesmen
become consultants, texts (minutes of planning meetings,
tenders, etc.) become as important as technical know-how,
and a medium which they must learn to negotiate, by piggy-
backing on the records of previous performance of their
colleagues.

Just where does such activity stand in relation to the Data
Protection Act? It does not involve 'holdings' of the sort
implied in the Act; it does not involve 'accuracy' or 'access'.
Where information profiles are extended into the wealth of
informal information (direct and indirect), which circulates in
any organisation — membership of professional organisations (especially where membership is non-compulsory and
where an employee's concerns can be gauged from affiliation

to special interest groups), membership of computer conferences, patterns of social exchange — the notion of privacy is difficult to sustain.

Policy on personal information processing in the context of work is currently framed by the demand side (the employer). Trade unions have, in many cases, been slow to appreciate the augmentation potential of new technology, though Delors' vision of a social contract across Europe has initiated use of networks by UK trade unionists. Another incipient area of networking is unionisation of oil workers, geographical need dictating the use of technology. Where unions have taken a stance on data protection and personal information, it has often been in the form of a guide to minimalist compliance with the Act, to prevent the release of information to those outside the organisation.

The problem of outsider access to personnel information is already apparent in areas where central government is seeking greater 'accountability' in local government service. School boards, and their equivalent in the health service, will have access to information on pupil progress and teaching performance, as part of a policy of informed choice. Policymakers have proposed an extension of this accountability into other areas of local government, with representatives of the consumer of services attending planning meetings, discussion of resource allocations and so on (Pollitt, 1988). Such proposals for accountable government can blow the cover of formal reporting protocols: the doctrine of collective responsibility will be difficult to sustain where individual contributions to policy can be identified and delineated.

Such proposals will only work where there is consensus on the benefits of participation. The training offered by employers in handling technology must incorporate an understanding of the extent and likely uses of information attached to individuals (from payroll number or PIN to textual or communication audit). Guidelines on company practice can enhance the benefits for both the demand and supply side in open exploitation of such information.

## Consumer information: the market is the massage

The main concerns of the public, according to the Fifth Report of the Data Registrar, in the area of consumer information, are direct mail and credit information (Data Protection Registrar, 1989, p. 4320/7). The resale of address lists, and resulting junk or unsolicited mail, has alerted public attention to potential abuses in the commercial sector of computerised personal information; a particular point of concern is the exploitation and resale of official or compulsory information, such as the contents of electoral registers and census returns, a well-established practice, which, as we have indicated, is held up by government as a model for commercial exploitation.

Trading of mailing lists is not exclusively a transfer of data from public to private sector; intra-commercial exchange is extensive (banks are major practitioners), and the emergence of common communication protocols will facilitate such activity. The purpose of such exchange will vary from context to context. In some cases, neutral mailing lists will provide data for massage and resale for market research; in others, a mailing list attached to a product or service may be sold to a company offering a related product or service; in others again, particularly in the finance and credit sector, data may be reused with little or no alteration. For companies where increased market share depends on product or service differentiation, mailing lists are hot commercial property, and exchange may constitute a breach of confidence. Companies which gain advantage from cost cutting may not regard their client lists as sensitive, however, and may be willing to share information for a price.

Control in these areas is likely to be achieved by the development of guidelines and codes of practice for different industrial sectors. The Data Registrar is committed to a policy of regulation by prescription; his office has issued drafts for some areas, and several professional bodies have produced codes. The first commercial draft code was for companies using ISTEL, an EDI-based integrated manufacturing package in which responsibility for personal data is localised at the level of the line manager. Other working codes appeared in 1986, produced by the Association of British Travel Agents and the Advertising Association (which coordinates activities

emanating from the Direct Marketing Industry). These have
been followed by the Association of Chief Police Officers, the
Committee of Vice-Chancellors and Principals, the British
Computing Society, the Institute of Personnel Management,
the Institute of Chartered Accountants, the Institute of Administrative Accountants, and the Local Authorities Management Services and Computer Committee (LAMSAC) (Data
Protection Registrar, 1987, Section 4. 193). The mailing prefer-
ence list is a protective mechanism which has emerged from
lobbying in this area, and the Registrar has persuaded several
key players to state openly that data supplied by members of
the public may be used for purposes other than the ostensible
reason for data input.

Data subjects have expressed concern about the divulging
or transfer of credit information, especially from the private to
the public sector, where it may be used as an indicator of
potential criminality, or to remove potential state benefits.
This preoccupation has not stunted the growth of a jungle of
financial services, or dampened consumer enthusiasm for
credit at point-of-sale facilities supplied by individual
retailers; the convenience for both supply and demand sides
outweighs potential invasion of privacy. This is, however, an
area where misinformation is prevalent, partly because many
credit agencies link an individual to previous addresses, and
the inhabitants of these addresses, whose credit record may in
some cases contaminate that of the data subject in question.

Data subjects place information on their personal shopping
habits, or their taste, low on the agenda for protection. They
might consider that such data are considered desirable by
compilers of police computerised databanks, as sudden acquisition of an expensive item may indicate ill-gotten gain, or
political sympathies may be derived from purchasing habits
(reading material or music are obvious indicators of affiliation). The use of accounts as an indicator of spending and
personal habits has a long pedigree as a tool for investigators,
fiscal, criminal, and other.

There is little need for benefit analysis in the context of
computerised personal information and consumerism; the
perceived dangers of direct abuse by data users are clearly
outweighed by the practical benefits to those whose personal
data are manipulated. Consumers can pluck from a cor-
nucopia of stylistic choice permitted by manipulation and

targeting of personal data. Electronic shopping (currently constrained in the home by lack of installed equipment) may be extended by the development of public access terminals, which will allow consumers to profile an individual style and match it with retailing resources.

One development in networked consumer information, which is taken very seriously by producers, is the user group, which is often a source of ready-made and detailed marketing data, on reactions to new products, service and maintenance. Many of the major computer manufacturers take their user groups on board at the early stages of product planning, which may be seen as a version of the accountability which we have discussed under the individual as employee.

Is the existing contingency approach to consumer data desirable, or even adequate? There is little possibility of regulating abuse of mailing lists, for example, by appeal to major legislation. The Data Protection Act, as we have emphasised, does not currently cover secondary use of data, and the Consumer Protection Act (1987) does not address this area. Extension of guidelines and codes of practice may be encouraged (and is being encouraged by the Data Registrar), but compliance with these will remain voluntary. We suspect that consumer data protection holds little interest for individuals, apart from the junk mail issue. Manipulation and massage is an intrinsic part of the market system, and there will be little pressure for policy changes, as long as the system delivers the goods.

## Personal information and leisure: tools for 'com-viviality'

The information which we consider in this section relates the data subject overtly to a group of his, or her, own choosing. It may be broadly classed as information attached to leisure or non-work activities which are serviced or represented by an outside individual or organisation (membership of religious groups, clubs, voluntary work), where further use of registered personal data is controlled by the group, or as information which is the unequivocal property of the data subject (where further use is totally in the subject's control). In the latter case, the Data Protection Act does not apply.

Some of the problems in this area are illustrated by the

exploitation of membership lists of clubs. These are covered by the Data Protection Act in terms of access and accuracy, but, of course, the use to which the data are put is not curtailed, though clubs should indicate likely further uses of data to their members. If a dating agency sells its client list to Club Mediterranée, the clients may be happy to see their hunting grounds extended; but if they are offered unsolicited specialist services, they may object. Some clubs (the sporting area is obviously relevant) may wish to sell their lists to commercial companies in return for sponsorship, and members who object may have to raise the issue as a point of business in club meetings. The problem is particularly piquant in the case of resale of local authority data which relate to leisure services. Where funds are limited, there may be potential sponsorship from companies selling products to niche markets identified from local authority files. Should a library service or swimming club seek such sponsorship?

The exchange of goods, skills and services on a one-to-one basis without the mediation of an organised club is another area where personal data feature in the leisure sector. This need not be the contractual exchange offered by self-employed persons, but may consist of informal sharing based on mutual interest. The data subject will choose where to shop window what is on offer, through a bulletin board or e-mail service.

Who should be responsible for the regulation of the contents of such personal services? Libertarians say the users of the services themselves, and in the case of closed user groups this will be what happens, as non-participants will be ignorant of what is communicated. A personal information service on a public community network poses problems, however, and, if a local authority is held responsible for the contents of a service, legislation like Clause 29 may constrain what may be exchanged. The closure of BT's Chatline is a measure of the limited potential of personal information exchange, where public pressure may be exerted on an existing regulatory body. And who is responsible for IDs on a network which attaches subscribers to minority services? There is concern in the UK about the proliferation of sleazelines, or erotic network services, which lie outside existing laws. The position in France, however, is different, where *messageries roses* are an important part of Télétel's revenue for Minitel, as 'listening to the signal traffic on Minitel is like putting a stethoscope to the

French soul' (Bird and Collins, 1990; Palframan, 1990; Rambali, 1990).

Many of these issues have been raised by full-blown community or recreational information networks in the USA. Services, like the Well in the Bay Area of San Francisco which cover anything from courtship to reviews of computer conferences, are accessed through a range of special interest groups. Most trading and exchange and barter takes place online, and, as the participants are highly idiosyncratic, the possibilities for sourcing mass marketing and direct mailing operations are limited; any marketing approaches are made directly on the system. Many of these online communities are deeply localised, which limits the potential for abuse. What is more threatening, in the US context, is potential federal infiltration, and the profiling of individuals as non-conformists, and therefore potentially subversive.

Two areas which might arouse similar concern are mentioned in the Fifth Report of the Registrar: football club membership, and use of library files. The Registrar is concerned that the proposals for registration and control of the movements of football fanatics must not be allowed to extend into a general monitoring of personal mobility; a topical example is the cooperation of travel agents and police in tracking the movements of fans travelling from Scotland to Italy for the World Cup matches of 1990. The Registrar is also concerned about requests from police for information on the reading habits of subscribers to library services, as an indicator of personal proclivities (a tactic attempted in the hunt for the Yorkshire Ripper, but blocked by the libraries concerned).

## Conclusions

We have looked at personal information held and handled by computerised systems in four contexts, which reflect the public roles of data subjects, the supply side of the personal data market. And we have suggested that the legislation which covers these areas favours, of necessity, the demand, or data user, side.

Successive reports from the Data Registrar suggest that providers of personal data, or data subjects, are on the whole indifferent to the fate of their details. There have been fewer invocations of the Data Protection Act than expected (though the Act is young). Just as we take our physical environment for granted (the work of the agencies who shape it is largely transparent), so most of us take our data environment for granted. We are not aware of the range of databanks over which our personal data are scattered, or of the strange plants which may germinate when data are combined. It is only when things go wrong, such as a case of credit refused because of mistaken identity through wrong appropriation of data, or the advent of unsolicited mail, that data protection is invoked.

The Data Registrar is aware of the limitations of his remit, but is confident that more comprehensive protection can be offered by the provision of sectoral guidelines agreed by both subjects and users in a given area. These may, however, simply hone the evasion mechanisms of users, as their likely focus is access and accuracy, not aggregation and manipulation. The protection of data subjects might be better served by a programme of education which examines relevant sectoral or departmental data holders from a perspective of the roles played in public and private life. Our sample of four public roles is only a starting-point.

The use of personal data is really a form of social intelligence, the capability of individuals and groups of any size (from workgroup to corporation) to sustain and exploit their position in a given community, be it business, administration, education, industry, or research. The search for comprehensive details on individuals, which can allow agents to have the upper hand, is an intrinsic part of any intelligence operation. Those involved must be able to gather, process, manipulate and distribute information which comes from disparate sources, in different formats and media and through a range of channels, and the constraint of the law (particularly privacy legislation) is likely to be weak. Secondary processing is an essential of the intelligence function as practitioners must be able to interpret and apply what they have found out, to make sense of it in a given context; these can emerge from experience of etiquette, codes and registers, all of which confer an ability to read between the lines. These skills are part of the portfolio of users in each of our four domains (government, work, the market and leisure); some

may have expertise in conventional information processing
and retrieval, some may be managers with an interest in
competitive intelligence, others may be active outside the
world of formalised information as mediators, extension
workers, advisors who exploit traditional and intuitive
patterns of communication and control, the aspects of personal information which we suggest should be taken more
seriously.

What we see in the trade-offs and interchanges of public use
of individual records is a kind of hide-and-seek. Though users
are required by law to state the use of the data gathered in the
first instance from subjects, it is not in their interest to have to
reveal to subjects the ulterior purposes of data collection; to
reveal these is to remove the element of surprise which is
necessary to trap a miscreant, or a new client for a product.
The perspective of the data user is primarily that of a macro-
analyst, dealing in trends, profiles, probabilities; data are
used to create a text or script which drives a strategy or a
policy, or reinforces ideology. The perspective of the data
subject is unashamedly specific and individualistic; she, or
he, supplies data often in the context of an immediate and
defined need (the need for a loan, the need for a driving
licence, the need to borrow books), and any attempt to access
data is similarly prompted by a specific event: refusal of
credit, failure to obtain a post which has been applied for.
Data are seen as tuples or records which are either accurate or
not, and which conform to a set of defined criteria (composed
of similar elements) which entitle, or do not entitle, the subject
to certain benefits.

To what extent is education likely to reconcile the two
pespectives? And at what level should education begin? The
Registrar regrets that his limited resources cannot extend to
as full an educational programme as he would wish. As a
Department of Information Science, we introduce our under-
graduates to this topic in the first semester; it is an area which
brings home to them the extent to which an individual *is* the
information held about him, or her, in most institutional
contexts, and the importance of awareness (of accuracy and of
secondary purposes) in supplying data in any context. The
topic is also covered in both our Master's courses, and has
been the subject of several dissertations.

But such coverage hardly addresses the problem; a few

librarians here, some information managers there, are not
going to transform the game. What might do that is new
technology of the integrative, auditing sort, which will make
it difficult for either side (users or subjects) to outwit the other,
by making it easier for both sides to see what the other is up
to:

> It would seem that greater openness and explanations, although
> they might initially alarm people, would in the longer term lead to
> increased trust and decreased concern, at least in relation to more
> straightforward uses and disclosures. (Data Protection Registrar,
> 1989, p. 4320/20[1])

Such an open information policy is unlikely, however, as long
as policy emanates from data users — the people or organisations who control the personal data — who currently have
the balance of power in their favour.

## Note

[1] The Third Report of the Data Protection Registrar (June 1987) and the Fifth
Report (June 1989) both appear in the *Encyclopedia of Data Protection* (1988),
which is updated as relevant material appears (see references).

## References

Baird, P., Cronin, B. and Davenport, L. (1989) 'Hypertext and adding
    value' in *Proceedings of a conference on Hypermedia/hypertext
    and object-oriented databases*, Brunel University; Unicom, pp.
    105–13.
Bartholomew, A. (1989) 'GOSIP — a practical guide to OSI pro-
    curement', *Telecommunications* (International edn.), **23**(11),
    November pp. 33–6.
Bird, J. and Collins, R. (1990) 'Children tune into computer porn by
    phone', *The Sunday Times*, 12 March.
Birkinshaw, P. (1987) in *Scottish Current Law Statutes*, Access to
    Personal Files Act, 1987 c. 37.
British Library (1989) 'Hypertext as a medium for computer-
    supported collaborative work', *BL R&DD Research Bulletin*, **4**(3).
Brown, R. (1987) 'The road to totalitarian freedom, and the Australia
    card', *Computer Law and Security Report*, Sep/Oct, pp. 8–11.
Campbell, D. (1986) *On the record*, London, Michael Joseph.
Data Protection Registrar, (1988) *Third Report of the Data Protection*

*Registrar* in S. Chalton and S. Gaskill, *Encyclopedia of Data Protection*, London, Sweet and Maxwell.

Data Protection Registrar (1988) *Fifth Report of the Data Protection Registrar*, June 1989, in S. Chalton and S. Gaskill. *Encyclopedia of Data Protection*, London, Sweet and Maxwell.

Davenport, L. and Cronin, B. (1987). 'Value-added re-selling and public domain data', *Electronic and Optical Publishing Review*, **7**(1), March, pp. 8–12.

Department of Trade and Industry (1986), *Government-held tradeable information: an introduction*, London, HMSO.

DG XIII, (1990) *Information Market*, **62**, May-June.

Frenchman, K. (1988) 'Tapping new resources as computers get to work'. *The Observer*, 29 June, *vi*.

Greenleaf, G. (1988) 'Lessons from the Australia Card: *deus ex machina*', *Computer Law and Security Report*, March/April, pp. 6–8.

Jones, M. (1986) 'Hacking — a weak precedent? A report on the Schifreen/Gold "hacking" trial', *Computer Law and Security Report*, May-June, pp. 14–16.

Judge, P. (1989) 'A profile of progress', *Systems International (UK)*, **1**(12), December, pp. 52–6.

Marx, G. T. (1990) 'The case of the omniscient organization', *Harvard Business Review*, March-April, pp. 12–30.

Palframan, D. (1990) 'Call for a clean image', *Management Today*, June, p. 120.

Pollitt, C. (1988) 'Bringing consumers into performance measurement', *Policy and Politics*, **16**(2), pp. 77–87.

Portman, E. C. P. (1988) 'The Alvey DHSS Large Demonstrator Project' in P. Duffin (ed.), *Knowledge based systems: applications in administrative government*, Chichester, Ellis Horwood.

Pounder, C. (1986) 'Police computers and the Metropolitan Police, Part III: data protection and the control of police computers', *Information Age*, **8**(1), January, p. 15.

Preston, R. J. (1988) 'The UK Government Data Network' in *Telecommunications — Network Planning and Management: proceedings of a conference*, London, 4–5 October, London, IBC Technical Services.

Rambali, P. (1990) *French Blues*, London, Minerva.

*Scottish Current Law Statutes*, Access to Personal Files Act 1987, c. 37.

Slatin, J. M. (1988) 'Hypertext and the teaching of writing', in E. Barrett, (ed.), *Text, context and hypertext*, Cambridge, MIT, pp. 111–29.

# CHAPTER 2

# Legal information for living: the role of information technology

## R. J. Hartley and John Williams

### Introduction

In this chapter, we discuss the current and potential uses of information technology in making legal information accessible to the general public. Initially it is helpful to make a crude distinction between legal information and legal advice. It is also necessary to draw distinctions between the various categories of people who use legal information ranging from lawyers to the general public. These issues are addressed in the first part of the chapter. Important as information technology is, it must be acknowledged that much legal information is transmitted to the general public by other means such as through a solicitor or by consulting a textbook. Thus the other channels through which the general public can access legal information are also considered. This is restricted to what might be termed formal channels of communication such as advice centres or legal publications. Informal sources such as neighbours or the person in the pub are excluded, though of course we recognise that they may be the most used of all. The various approaches to the use of information technology in making legal information accessible are then discussed. It should be noted that to date most uses of information technology in the field of legal information have been in the presentation of legal information to legal professionals or para-professionals. Finally the chapter speculates on possible developments in the use of information technology in making legal information more readily accessible to the general public. In illustrating the case, reference is made only to English and Welsh law, but since information technology knows no national boundaries the application of information technology to the dissemination of legal information is not confined to England and Wales. Whilst seeking to demonstrate the pervasiveness of the law in everyday affairs, examples of legal matters are wherever possible limited to an area of common concern, namely divorce. This is a common use of the law by the general public and there are many occasions when professional legal advice is not used.

## Living with the law

Public awareness of legal issues is unfortunately at a very low level. This may be partly explained by the failure to include law as part of the school curriculum. At the further education level very few students opt to take law at A level, whereas in higher education law is chosen mainly by those who want to become either solicitors or barristers. However, the lack of awareness must also be a consequence of the belief that law does not really affect the general public other than in exceptional cases such as house sale, dismissal from employment or a criminal offence. In those situations, lay people are likely to consult a lawyer rather than attempting to do the work themselves. However, this view is misleading and underestimates the number of legal settings which arise in everyday life. Thus it is common to hear people say that they have no knowledge or experience of the law of contract. Contracts are, it is generally thought, agreements made in writing and couched in highly legalistic language. This is not the case. Our daily affairs lead us to make many unwritten contracts with, for example, supermarkets, bus companies and garages. Similarly, many of the skirmishes that people have will invariably have legal dimensions. A row with a neighbour about late night parties may give rise to both criminal and civil law issues.

Law regulates most areas of life. It is therefore important that we recognise the legal dimension of problems and classify them as such. So, for example, tripping on an uneven paving stone may be classified by the injured party seeking compensation as a political question and help may be sought from a local councillor. In fact it is a legal obligation that makes the responsible authority liable for any injury caused and a claim would be best pursued through legal rather than political procedures. Making lay people aware of the legal dimension is one of the first obstacles to be overcome when considering how best to help people help themselves. Increasing awareness of legal issues can be achieved through current affairs programmes, broadcasting of Parliamentary debates on law reform and books of general legal interest. Attention is also drawn to legal matters through a wide variety of other publications which contain a legal column or occasional articles on legal matters. Thus newspapers such as *The Independent,* the *Guardian,* the *Daily Telegraph* and *The Times* contain regular law reports and features. Many magazines also carry articles on legal topics and/or offer help and advice columns. Some examples are *Cosmopolitan, Family Circle, House Beautiful* and *Living.* The consumer magazine *Which?* is also a regular source of advice and information. A number of the tabloid newspapers also have a legal advice section. Through such publications and the work of various pressure groups people are becoming more aware of their legal rights and duties. However, there is still much work to be done and people in this country are nowhere near as law conscious as their American counterparts.

When considering legal material four potential markets can be identified. These are the legal profession, 'para-legal' professionals, advice agencies (other than the professional lawyer) and the general public. The legal profession is a market in which certain assumptions can be made. For example, lawyers are trained in the use of source material such as case law and statutes. They have the basic skills of interpretation and application in addition to a detailed understanding of how the legal system works. Para-legals are those professionals who are required to have a detailed understanding of how the law applies to their own profession. Included in this category are teachers, environmental health officers, social workers, hoteliers, farmers, doctors and

retailers. Their primary knowledge relates to their own professions, but in consequence of their training they are aware
of the general and specific legal regulation of their work. This
group presents a challenge to the publisher. Assumptions
cannot be made. What approach should be adopted? Is it
necessary to provide a specialist range of material for the
para-legals, or is it better to let them rely on the traditional
lawyer's market? Advice centres using non-lawyers may face
similar problems to the para-legals. The specialised advice
centres (Women's Aid, Housing Aid, National Council for
Civil Liberties) require of their advisers detailed knowledge of
the relevant area, which in itself may be very broad. For
example, an adviser for Women's Aid might be required to
know the law relating to divorce, family property, social
security, financial provision and child custody. General
advice centres (Citizens' Advice Bureaux, student unions) face
the problems of having to cover a wide range of topics which
forces them to address the question of how much depth is
necessary or feasible.

Individual members of the public provide a very complex
market. It is highly varied in terms of the skills it possesses
and the problems which it presents. Individuals start with the
disadvantage of not having any framework within which to
operate and will invariably have been denied the training
facilities and the related support services available to the
other groups. They will also be denied the benefit of experience in dealing with similar issues.

The vast quantity of published legal information can be
categorised in a variety of ways. In the first place it can be
divided into primary and secondary sources. Primary sources
include Acts of Parliament and reported decisions of courts
and tribunals. This material is the province of the lawyer and
on rare occasions, possibly, the other professionals who have
contact with the law as a part of their work, for example
accountants or the medical profession. Secondary material is
not the formal record of law but consists of material such as
digests of cases, encyclopaedic summaries of various aspects
of the law, textbooks and monographs about particular parts
of the law and journals containing discussions of law. Again
these are written with the lawyer as the intended audience but
some of this material will be of interest to other professionals
and to advice and aid workers such as social workers and

Citizens' Advice Bureaux.

People have need to consult the law for one or two reasons: they may be seeking either information or advice. Information is general in nature, not related to any specific personal problem or issue, and educative in its objective. Advice is more specific, it relates to a particular personal problem or issue and it is functional in objective. So, for example, people may seek information on the law relating to libel in order to better understand newspaper reports of a recent *Private Eye* libel case. However, if they suspect that they have been libelled advice will be sought on the specific publication in order to discover whether or not it damages their reputation. This distinction is crude and it may be more accurate to describe them as being the two extremes of a spectrum. A person listening to the Jimmy Young show may learn of the success of a holiday-maker in obtaining a partial refund from the tour operator in respect of an unsatisfactory package holiday. Although this is information, it does have elements of advice because that person's own circumstances coincide, more or less, with those of the successful complainant. Nevertheless, in order to pursue the matter he/she will require more specific advice which takes into consideration the peculiarities of his/her own experience. The distinction does, however, have implications for those preparing guides for lay people. The expectation of a general educative guide may be different from those designed to assist lay people in actually representing themselves before an industrial tribunal.

## Accessibility of the law

Accessibility of the law refers to both physical and intellectual accessibility. By physical accessibility is meant the access to the primary literature of the law such as Acts of Parliament. For most lay people, the lack of physical access to the law will be a considerable impediment. In general it is only likely to be those individuals who live in the larger cities and know how to make use of well equipped reference libraries who will be able to see the material. It is most unlikely that the typical person will purchase a copy of an Act of Parliament. It is probably in the area of physical accessibility to the law that information technology has so far contributed most and can be expected to contribute most in future.

In addition to physical accessibility, there is the problem of intellectual accessibility of the law, that is to say the extent to which a legal document can be understood by a lay person. The intellectual accessibility of law to lay people depends to a large extent upon the way in which that law is stated by the lawmaker. Acts of Parliament are usually unintelligible due to the manner in which they are drafted. Much legislation causes trained lawyers considerable difficulty in interpretation; it is, therefore, unrealistic to assume that lay people will find statutes a useful guide to the law. However, the complexity of a statute may vary depending upon the nature of the subject matter. For example, tax statutes are drafted very precisely with numerous cross-references. Section 7 of the Finance Act 1989 reads as follow:

(1) Section 38(1) of the Vehicle (Excise) Act 1971 shall be amended as follows.
(2) Before the definition of 'conditional sale agreement' there shall be inserted 'community bus' means a vehicle used on public roads solely in accordance with a community bus permit (within the meaning of the Traffic Act 1985), and not used for providing a service under an agreement providing for service subsidies (within the meaning of s.63(10)(b) of that Act).

This does not provide a definition of 'community bus' which is immediately of use to the reader. A trained lawyer dealing with this definition for the first time will be able to work out the meaning using basic legal skills. To the legal expert in the law on community buses the meaning will probably be self-explanatory. However, for lay people the definition will cause considerable difficulty. Contrast this with the relatively simple language of the Children Act 1989 which defines 'parental responsibility' as 'all the rights, duties, powers, responsibilities and authority which by law a parent of a child has in relation to the child and his property' (see Children Act 1989 s.3(1)). In neither case are lay people provided with an easily understandable definition. Thus entering 'community bus' or 'parental responsibility' in the statute file of LEXIS, a major commercial legal database (see below), or looking at the Acts in the 1989 volume of the statutes, would not really help lay people pursuing an enquiry into either of these concepts. Even the more reader-friendly language of the Children Act 1989 raises a number of questions such as what are those rights etc. which by law the parent has? How is the concept of parental responsibility used in the 1989 Act? Does a local authority assume exclusive parental authority when it has a child in care? How does the *Gillick* v. *West Norfolk and Wisbech Area Health Authority* case ([1986] AC 112) fit into this statutory definition? The wording has to be considered in the context of the statute and subject to the 'rules' of statutory interpretation. Nevertheless, the gentler language in the Children Act 1989 does have implications for those charged with producing guides for non-lawyers. Law depends to a large extent on the precise use of language. It is desirable that lay people using the law should, so far as is possible, be acquainted with the text of the primary material, namely statutes and cases. This is an easier task when using the language in the Children Act 1989 rather than that in the Finance Act of the same year.

The Children Act 1989 provides an interesting illustration of this point. To a large extent the implementation of the Act will be the responsibility of social workers. Legal training of social workers varies, both at the academic and in-service stages (see Ball *et al.*, 1988). In its guide to the Children Act the Department of Health makes the claim that 'the Act has been drafted in a clear style which should make it accessible to non-lawyers' (Department of Health, 1989). This may be a somewhat optimistic claim for the legislation; Parliament still has a long way to go before it produces legislation which can be understood by lawyer and lay people alike. Nevertheless, when explaining the concept of 'parental responsibility' to a social worker greater uses can be made of the wording of the Act than would the case if it followed the drafting pattern of the Finance Act 1989. This also applies to parents whose children have been taken into care under a care order. In such circumstances the local authority has a duty to inform the parents, or persons who have parental responsibility for the child, of the legal consequences of the order. Usually this is done by way of an explanatory leaflet written with lay people in mind. The wording of section 3(1) of the Children Act 1989 could actually be used in such a leaflet together with examples of parental rights, powers, duties, responsibilities and authority which parents have under the law.

Less paraphrasing is required when explaining the Children Act 1989. Indeed it would make much sense to use the wording of section 3(1) as the starting-point of the explanation. This is important, as the less the person producing the guide has to resort to his/her own interpretation the closer the reader will be to the wording of the Act and therefore the better able to explore, exploit and use any discretion the Act gives. This is the approach adopted by the Department of Health's Introduction. A similar exercise in relation to Finance Act 1989 s.7 would require the author to depart much more from what the Act actually says, thus to greater generality and less precision.

## Using the law

The public perception of law is that it provides most, if not all, of the answers to whatever particular problem may arise in daily living. A great deal is expected of law and people are both surprised and resentful when they realise that law has limitations. When seeking advice whether from a professional lawyer, an advice centre or a legal publication, lay people invariably expect confirmation of their own view as to what the law should be, rather than a statement of what the law actually is. At times the advice giver is presented with the response 'that cannot be right, it is so unfair, you don't know what you are talking about'. Thus it is essential that advice when given, and in whatever form it is given, recognises the expectations of the advice seeker. This is important and influences the manner in which advice should be made available to the recipient.

Another difficulty which must be confronted is the fact that law does not fall into convenient and discrete groups. Subject boundaries are nothing more than convenient headings under which law can be taught; they have little to do with actual practice. So, for example, a person seeking a divorce will have to consider not only the law of divorce, but also that which applies to taxation, property transfer, ownership of property and child custody. A guide on the mechanics of divorce may be inadequate for this purpose.

Advice on the law, in order to be of practical use, must be

placed in a particular context. Thus a person seeking advice
on divorce can be advised that a petition may be based upon
what is referred to as 'unreasonable behaviour'. The meaning
of this concept may also be explained and examples given.
The recipient may feel in full possession of all the relevant law
and therefore competent to act in divorce proceedings. However, such information on its own may raise false hopes and
may mislead. Firstly, the advice must be placed in a procedural context. How are applications for divorce made?
Fortunately, undefended divorce petitions may now be presented under the 'special procedure' — a somewhat deceptive
nomenclature as 98 per cent of all divorces are obtained in this
way. A number of specialist guides are available to assist
people using this procedure in addition to the one issued by
the county court office. Problems arise, however, where the
other party decides to contest the divorce proceedings, as is
often the case at the outset of the divorce process. At this stage
the general knowledge that may be required to complete a
'user-friendly' form for the special procedure proves to be
inadequate where litigation may be possible. It will be necessary to seek advice on procedural matters such as time-limits
for the presentation of the petition, the method of serving
documents and the manner in which to respond to a cross-
petition.

Secondly, lay people will have to consider the implications
of the law of evidence. For everyday purposes a person can be
persuaded to believe that a particular event occurred by the
use of what a court of law may regard as unreliable evidence.
Hearsay evidence ('Jones told me that Smith is having an
affair with Evans') is generally not acceptable by the courts,
whereas in everyday life we may be prepared to accept the
veracity of what Jones told the speaker. Opinion evidence ('I
think Smith is having an affair because he seems the type of
person who does that sort of thing') is similarly regarded as
being unreliable. Why should one person's opinion, or prejudice, carry any weight in determining the truth? It is also
necessary to weigh up the strength of the evidence and how it
will stand up before the court. Such considerations are important in determining whether or not a case is worth contesting.
Thus in divorce proceedings it is difficult to decide whether to
contest a petition based on unreasonable behaviour — would
the evidence in the petition be sufficient to satisfy a court? A

guide, in order to be effective, must convey such information to the user as well as the substantive law on the subject.

Thirdly, lay people must have some awareness of 'the way in which lawyers think'. This is a vague concept, but nevertheless it is important that its existence is at least recognised. Partly this reflects the lawyers' dispassionate and objective approach in assessing evidence. Professional lawyers can step back from the case and consider what facts are relevant and what are irrelevant for the purposes of the law. Lay people conducting their own cases may at times find it difficult to separate their emotions and commitment to the case from what is hard evidence which will be acceptable by the courts. It also includes the lawyers' understanding of the tactics of conducting a legal dispute. In many instances such considerations are offensive in so far as they perpetuate the exclusive character of the profession by discouraging lay people. However, they do come into operation so it is helpful if a person contemplating self-representation in divorce proceedings is aware of how the legal representative for the other party will be thinking.

Finally, it is necessary to give the recipient of advice a basic understanding of legal methodology. Of particular importance is development of the law by the judiciary. How important are the courts in interpreting legislation? To what extent do the judges actually make law? What is the binding system of precedent? What is the *ratio decidendi* of a case and why is it important? These are important concepts because they influence the way in which the court will respond to a previous judicial decision. When attempting to prove desertion in divorce proceedings the petitioner must show an intention to desert and factual separation. The relevance of the cases of *Perry* v. *Perry* ([1963] 3 All ER 766) and *Hopes* v. *Hopes* ([1949] P 227) must be appreciated in order to understand the law better.

It is also necessary to have an understanding of the manner in which statutory discretions are exercised. When an Act gives the court a broad discretion (for example, in the redistribution of property and income after divorce), how will it be used? What restraints, if any, are imposed? In what way do earlier judicial decisions help in predicting how the court will act?

The above matters may appear to act as a disincentive to

lay people to act for themselves when dealing with their legal
affairs. However, in the case of the non-legal professional
such matters will not be allowed to deter as that person will be
charged with performing specified duties under the law. For
lay people there may be advantages of cost, speed and control
in conducting their own legal case. In some instances, such as
hearings before Industrial Tribunals, the legal system positively encourages self-representation. Lay people seeking to
conduct their own divorces should be encouraged and given
the broader range of advice necessary to enable them to
compete with professional lawyers.

## Traditional sources of legal advice and information

### Printed sources

The secondary material noted earlier can also be categorised
according to the intended audience. Many books and
encyclopaedias are intended for the legal profession. Some
will be introductory texts intended for the student lawyer,
such as I. R. Storey's *Conveyancing* (Butterworths, 1983),
whilst others are standard reference works for practitioners in
that particular legal field such as *Williams' Contract for sale
of land and title to land* (4th edn. by G. Battersby Butterworths, 1975, and 4th cumulative supplement, 1983). Such
material will be of value to the experienced aid worker or
professional from a related field but will only be of interest to
the most dedicated and determined member of the general
public. This material, together with the primary literature,
will not be discussed in detail in this chapter and the interested reader should consult Logan (1986) for further guidance
in this subject.

A further category of book material is the introduction to a
particular aspect of the law for professionals from other fields.
One example of this type of publication is Ruth Lister's
*Welfare benefits* (Sweet & Maxwell, 1981) which is meticulous,
clearly written and relatively free of jargon. *Essential law for
social workers* by Gwyneth Roberts and published by Oyez in
1981 details the powers and responsibilities of social service
departments. Similarly, *Social services law* and *The law of
mental health* by John Williams (Fourmat, 1988 and 1990)

provide practising social workers with a guide to the law.
These books may be more accessible to the lay people, but it
should be noted that they should not be construed as light
reading.

Finally, there is a large number of books on legal matters
aimed at the general public. Given the complexity of the law
and the need for professional advice on its interpretation in
any specific situation, this is somewhat surprising. None the
less, the continuing appearance of such material in the lists of
books published by conventional publishers and published by
the various advice centres and pressure groups demonstrates
a continuing need for and interest in such material.

There are a number of popular guides to all aspects of the
law which are likely to be of interest to the general public.
Probably the most accessible of these are *Which? Guide to
your rights* published in 1980 for the Consumers' Association
by Hodder and Stoughton and the *Penguin guide to the Law*
edited by Pritchard and published by Allen Lane in 1982. *You
and your rights: an A-Z guide to law* (7th edn., Readers Digest
Association, 1984) uses an alphabetic arrangement of legal
topics for lay people, but some degree of legal knowledge is
probably necessary to make best use of the arrangement. For
example, it is important to be able to categorise a problem
broadly according to its legal classification before intelligent
use of such guides is possible. *Everyman's own lawyer* by 'A.
Barrister' (71st edn., Macmillan, 1981) offers a somewhat
heavier reference guide for the lay public. The pamphlet
*Coping with the system: a brief citizen's manual* by R. Leach
(Interaction/National Extension College, 1980) is a quick
guide and reference tool which is aimed at both school-leavers
and immigrants. The language has been tested on a number
of people for whom English is the second language.

Further books for lay people cover some section of the law
such as consumer rights or women's rights. An example of a
book in the former area is *Consumers Know Your Rights* by J.
Harries (Oyez Longman, 1983). Predictably this area of law is
well served by a series of publications from the Consumers'
Association such as *Law for consumers; Law for motorists*
and *Travelling consumer*. One well established example on
the subject of women's rights is Coote and Gill's *Women's
rights: a practical guide* (3rd edn., Allen Lane, 1981).

The complexity of rights in the fields of welfare and social security is amply demonstrated by the plethora of guides in this area. *Rights guide to non-means-tested social security benefits* by J. Luba and M. Rowland from the Child Poverty Action Group reached its tenth edition in 1987 whilst the same publishers' *National Welfare Benefits handbook* reached its twelfth edition in 1982. Tony Lynes, *The Penguin guide to social security benefit*, 4th edition, was published by Allen Lane in 1981. There are other general guides and also books and booklets about particular problems such as disability rights (the annual *Disability rights handbook* from the Disability Alliance), single parents (*Single and pregnant* from the National Council for One Parent Families) and homelessness (*Supplementary Benefits for single homeless people* from the Campaign for Single Homeless People).

Clearly the law is not static and published commentaries are out of date almost before they are published. One method of attempting to overcome this is by use of loose-leaf encyclopaedias which are updated at regular intervals. One example is the *Encyclopaedia of social services law and practice* from the publisher Sweet & Maxwell. A very well established publication which is available in many public libraries as well as advice centres is *CANS* (*Citizens' Advice Notes Service*) which provides a digest of legislation over a wide range of matters and is available from the National Council for Voluntary Organizations. Journals and newsletters are available which cover recent legal developments in a given field. Examples are *Law Centre News* and *LAG Bulletin*. These publications are essentially aimed at advice centres rather than individuals, although they do attract a number of individual subscribers with an interest in this area of law.

In addition to the large number of books and booklets there is a vast range of leaflets and pamphlets explaining the legal rights of individuals in many spheres of human activity. These leaflets are produced by various government departments such as the Department of Employment, the Department of Social Security or the Department of the Environment, and by other government bodies such as the Equal Opportunities Commission. Many local authority departments also produce a range of leaflets covering, for example, housing benefits. Leaflets are also produced by trades unions especially in the areas of employment rights and health and safety matters. Numerous campaigning organisations such as Child Poverty Action Group and Shelter are also sources of leaflets. Similarly, law centres and advice centres produce a wide range of leaflets. Some of these leaflets may be brief and simple guides such as *Students and the community charge* from the Welsh Office or the Inland Revenue's *Income Tax and students*. Others are more substantial and informative booklets such as *Regulated tenancies* from the Department of the Environment. Yet others are very substantial and informative, for example, two pamphlets on pension choices from the Department of Social Security. Commercial publishers also produce this type of guide; for example, *Acting in person . . . How to obtain an undefended divorce* published by Oyez.

Finding out about this massive amount of information is no simple task. A brief starting-point is provided by Bull (1986). However the major source is the excellent *Know how to find out your rights* by Morby (1982). This provides informative annotations about each item listed and is not afraid to make recommendations of items for purchase or those which can be avoided. Whilst the book is intended for advice centre workers, it will be of considerable interest to many lay people who can profitably consult it in their local libraries.

Other branches of the media are well established in providing access to legal information and advice of a general nature. There is a regular legal advice spot on the *Jimmy Young Programme* on Radio Two, for example. Feature programmes about legal matters currently in the news will regularly appear on the television. These tend to be specific themes or progammes such as the legal position regarding compensation for hospital negligence. Such programmes do not offer advice services for viewers with particular problems. A more recent development is the availability of advice services over the telephone on matters concerned with consumer, financial or personal affairs. An example of such a service is Advice Call which is offered by Air Call Medical Services of Milton Keynes.

### Advice services

Advice centres have played a prominent part in making the law more accessible to the public. Whereas many people will feel intimidated by going to a solicitor in private practice for legal advice, they may be willing to go a CAB or to a neighbourhood law centre. Very often such centres are better informed on certain areas of law than solicitors in private practice. This is particularly true of welfare law and housing matters. Funding of such centres is often uncertain. Nevertheless, they provide an invaluable service and their role is likely to increase with the government's changes in the Legal Aid scheme.

Many public libraries have chosen in recent years to develop what they refer to as community information services. These are based upon the premises that the public library service is available to all and that the traditional book-based reference service offered by many libraries is inappropriate for many of the potential clientele, in particular people from a disadvantaged group. In this context 'disadvantaged' are viewed as those who belong to lower socio-economic groups or who are disadvantaged through an inability to obtain, understand or act upon information that affects their lives. The services themselves are concerned with providing information to help resolve daily problems. It is clear that this role could overlap that of many of the advice-giving agencies and even the work of numerous professional groups including lawyers and social workers. In practice, many libraries operate in close cooperation with the advice-giving agencies, on many occasions offering them premises in which to hold their surgeries. In addition, librarians have tended to eschew the giving of advice in particular situations and to concentrate upon the presentation of information, such as leaflets and pamphlets, or acting in a referral capacity directing people towards the relevant advice-giving agency. Furthermore, libraries have tended to develop a wider interpretation of what is meant by community information so that they will often offer a diary of forthcoming events in the locality as well as maintaining a database of advice-giving agencies and a selection of leaflets in welfare rights. There are numerous examples where information technology has been implemented in the furtherance of these community information services such as the development of local databases of contact people and organisations. More ambitiously, Devon County Libraries, through their PIRATE (Public Information In Rural Areas Technology Experiment) project have sought to use not only locally created databases but have experimented with the use of user-friendly interfaces in the interrogation of the databases and the use of telecommunications networks for the linking of geographically separated libraries (Dover, 1988).

## Technology and legal advice and information

The use of information technology to gain access to legal information is well established in two main areas, namely access to commercial databases of legal information and microcomputer-based 'consultation' systems, which offer information about specific legal problems such as tax calculation or benefit rights. It is premature to call these latter systems expert or intelligent systems, but steps are being taken in that direction too.

Ferret Information Systems specialise in the production of a software which calculates welfare rights benefits in a wide range of areas. The Maximiser program calculates entitlements to income support, family credit, housing benefit, child benefit, one-parent benefit, guardians allowance, attendance allowance, severe disablement allowance, mobility allowance, dental and optical charges and free or reduced prescription charges. Another product, Helper-PC, calculates entitlements to family credit, income support, rate rebate and community charge (poll tax) rebates. Other products calculate benefits for people returning to work (In-work Helper), or renovation grants entitlements (Renovator). Some of the packages come with an option to purchase, for an annual fee, updates to the product to take account of changes in the law and/or benefit entitlements. The packages are available for IBM PCs and in some cases for a wider range of equipment including Macintosh and Apricot micros and the hand-held Psion Organizer. Generally the packages are intended for use by advice agencies or, in some cases, government officers and the interface assumes that the user of the software is working on behalf of a client. The packages operate by asking a series of questions about the circumstances of the potential claimant and the outcome of a consultation is a calculation of the person's benefit entitlement. There are some occasions when attention is drawn to the relevant legislation. The operation of

the packages is sufficiently straightforward so that many
people will be capable of using them without the aid of an
advice worker and some public libraries are now making them
available for public use.

Commercial databases are intended almost exclusively for
the use of lawyers and related professionals such as accountants rather than for lay people. Such systems were first
developed in the early 1970s in the United States, but it was
probably not until 1980 that they became available in Great
Britain. Generally they provide access to the full text of
primary legal materials, that is Acts of Parliament, statutory
instruments and decisions of courts and tribunals. Some
databases confine themselves to those cases which are
published in the recognised law reports, such as the *All
England* or the *Weekly Law Reports*. Others also include a
number of otherwise unreported cases. For example, LEXIS
includes agency transcripts of cases which never actually
reach the law reports. This can cause problems as the courts
may be unwilling to accept as authority a decision that is only
reported on a database such as LEXIS. It also adds to the bulk
of material which the adviser may feel constrained to consult
when giving advice. The secondary literature is less in
evidence in such commercial search services but even here
developments are occurring. The two major systems are both
American, namely LEXIS and Westlaw, the former containing a large amount of British and European legal information. However there are now a wide range of services
available and substantial portions of the law of many countries in Europe are now accessible in machine readable form.
Details of these databases can be obtained from Raper (1988)
which lists some 35 databases containing legal material. One
interesting feature of online access to legal information is that
such information is not restricted to 'legal databases' but
many databases in other subjects include legal information.
For example, the database *CHILD ABUSE AND NEGLECT*
which is available from the large American search service,
Dialog, whilst primarily being a bibliographic database relating to research materials on child abuse and neglect also
includes (American) state statutes relating to child abuse and
neglect. A detailed exposition on databases intended for legal
professionals is not the purpose of this chapter and interested
readers can get further information from Bull (1986a) and

from Gray (1988), whilst those interested in the process of searching online databases should consult the recent text by Hartley *et al.* (1990).

The best example of information technology most readily accessible to the lay person is probably broadcast teletext services such as Ceefax from the BBC and Oracle from IBA with an installed user base in Great Britain of somewhere over 3 million sets. However these services are used almost exclusively for entertainment and transient information such as news, sports results and weather forecasts. They do not appear to offer any legal information.

British Telecom's interactive videotex service, Prestel, was designed and envisaged as a mass market interactive computerised information service. It now has a subscriber base of over 75,000; nevertheless, many of these are business or commercial subscribers and so it has not lived up to the initial expectations as a means of delivering information for living into the home. There is a small amount of legal advice and information available; for example, it is possible for the lay person to discover what to do if the cancellation of a direct debit to a bank is proving to be difficult. It is also possible to discover where in the government machine to turn for advice and information regarding immigration and nationality issues. There is also a certain amount of information relevant to the legal side of running a small business. However much of the information lacks depth and is often little more than an electronic referral service; in some cases the information offered is less detailed than can be acquired from a printed source. In addition to the fact that the information lacks depth is the problem that the coverage of information is also patchy. Thus it was not possible, at the time of writing, to find information about conveyancing or divorce or welfare benefits which are likely to be very common legal information and advice requirements.

In addition to the publicly available information which can be accessed by all users of Prestel, more restricted services are available on a subscription basis. These are known as Closed User Groups (CUGs). There is one well established CUG for law, namely LAWTEL, which is probably suitable for advice agencies such as Citizens' Advice Bureaux and voluntary and grant-aided organisations. LAWTEL contains summaries of all significant decisions, statutes, damage awards, bills going through Parliament, updates of statutory instruments and some other legal material. LAWTEL also provides an interactive research bureau. There is a small-scale demonstration of LAWTEL services available as a part of the public Prestel service.

Many local authorities have developed in-house viewdata services which are being used both to promote the authority and its activities in a more dynamic manner than has occurred previously and as a tool for providing elements of the community information that were mentioned earlier. Thus it is often possible to discover details of local sources of information and advice. Whilst most of these services are offered within the confines of council premises, some authorities are experimenting with the presentation of local videotex services in shopping precincts and in one case within a hotel foyer.

Electronic mail and bulletin board systems offer communication facilities which may aid the flow of legal information or make legal advice givers more accessible. For example, the LAWTEL research bureau mentioned earlier is accessible by Prestel's electronic mail service. One American lawyer has reported that the use of the Compuserve bulletin board, initially as a hobbyist, has resulted in his contacting numerous clients (Wallace, 1987).

A number of legal publications aimed at the professional lawyer are now appearing in the CD-ROM medium. Some are bibliographic databases, such as the Index to Legal Periodicals which lists the contents of some 500 law periodicals since 1981 and is updated quarterly. Others are primary legal material such as the Annual updates of the Swiss Federal Court since 1960 which contain the text of decisions in civil, commercial and taxation cases. Other European countries, including France, Holland, Austria and, most notably, Italy, have some CD-ROM products available in either trial or full production. The JUSTIS CD-ROM is based on the European Communities online database CELEX. It contains the legal information of the European Communities, that is to say the Treaties, Regulations and directives together with case law and preparatory work associated with the Communities' legal framework. It seems reasonable to suppose that similar products will emerge in Britain in the not too distant future. Whilst these products are intended for the lawyer, it seems at least possible that when CD-ROM becomes available for the domestic market, a compendium of legal information for lay people may be produced. This may not be far away given that computer games and the Guinness *Book of Records* are already available on CD-ROM. CD-ROM is probably also a very good delivery mechanism for providing digested legal information to the advice agencies and other legal para-professionals. Of course the main problem here is that of updating. It may be necessary to refer to traditional material to see whether there have been any developments since the last update of the CD-ROM.

Much excitement has been generated by the development of a new type of software called hypertext, initially in the shape of Hypercard on the Apple Macintosh but more recently with a spate of similar products intended for IBM micros and clones. Simply put, hypertext is a tool for creating associative links between discrete blocks of data. Thus, whereas in most books the presentation of the text is in a linear order, hypertext provides a mechanism for creating links between blocks of text so that they can be explored in an order which is not linear. One analogy would be with a thesaurus. This creates links between words with associated meanings and enables the user to move between those words regardless of where the user enters the thesaurus. The thesaurus would not be read from cover to cover. Hypertext provides a similar flexibility of information organisation and access. If the system can handle graphic and sound data as well as conventional text it provides a powerful tool for presenting information to a wide variety of people, and in this case it is referred to as 'hypermedia'. One of the major applications of hypertext to date has been in the production of a browsable guide to 'Glasgow Online' which was produced at Strathclyde University for the Glasgow Garden Festival (Baird, MacMorrow and Hardman, 1988). Work is now under way at the same institution to examine the feasibility of using hypertext systems to present legal information. In the first instance a system will be developed to present copyright law. There will be special emphasis on the application of the law to new information products and services. The system will be tested on law students and both law and information professionals (MacMorrow, 1990). Given the enthusiasm for hypertext systems it is important to note that it has not been demonstrated that it is any more effective than conventional retrieval systems in presenting information to professionals. Nevertheless, the success of the Glasgow Online project with its very diverse user population may lead to the conjecture that hypertext systems may prove very successful as a means of presenting legal information to lay people.

Computer assisted learning (CAL) or computer assisted instruction has been introduced on a small scale into British legal education but it is much more prevalent in American law schools. Some authors (e.g. Sparkes (1989)) have produced CAL programs using conventional high-level programming languages such as Pascal. Other researchers have produced packages using authoring systems, that is development environments specifically designed for creating CAL packages. These consist of facilities for the creation of screens and the linking of screens and the testing of learner responses against expected answers. The capability for the learner to work through the program at the learner's rather than the teacher's pace, and to move through branches of the program according to the responses to particular questions provides an apparently flexible method of learning. One authoring system, LEXICAL, has been designed specifically for use in computer assisted legal learning. It is a program designed to be used by people without computing skills and it is intended that it be widely used within law schools in the United Kingdom. Experience with CAL has largely been in the training of student lawyers, that is, legal professionals. An example is Sparkes' program for presenting the Matrimonial Homes Act 1983. More recently attempts have been made to use LEXICAL to produce packages to train para-legal professionals such as social workers in parts of the law relevant to them. A particular piece of legislation that lends itself to such projects is the Mental Health Act 1983, a knowledge of which is essential for approved social workers. The use of CAL is particularly valuable in rural areas where organising central training on a regular basis may prove to be expensive. If CAL can be used successfully to enable para-legal professionals to become acquainted with relevant aspects of the law, it is possible to hypothesise that the technology could also be used to bring legal information and legal training to lay people. Thus it might be possible to produce a tutorial program enabling a member of the general public to learn how to purchase a house or how to obtain a divorce. A more serious constraint on the development of such packages is a viable method of making them available to the person in the street.

It has been argued that CAL has failed to live up to expectations in that its uptake is not as widespread as its enthusiasts had hoped. It is argued that this is partly due to the inherent problems in CAL caused by the restrictions placed on the learning experience by the particular authoring system used to develop the package. More recently it has been suggested that more flexible and 'intelligent' learning packages could be produced by the integration into CAL of some of the techniques of artificial intelligence with the aim of producing intelligent tutoring or intelligent computer assisted learning package (Williams, 1989). This is seen by some people as a development of great promise, but it might be noted that this initial enthusiasm is remarkably similar to the enthusiasms shown for many developments related to the application of information technology and the optimism has yet to be borne out in practice. None the less attempts are being made to use intelligent tutoring techniques for legal training (Jones, 1989).

Mention of artificial intelligence leads logically to a consideration of the potential role of expert systems in making legal information more accessible. An expert system can be viewed as a computer program which emulates the advice offered by an acknowledged human expert in a particular situation. In many cases it may also seek to mimic the reasoning processes by which the human expert reached a conclusion about a particular problem. Some classic examples of successful pioneering expert systems are the medical diagnosis expert system, MYCIN, the geological prospecting system, PROSPECTOR, and the computer system configuration system, XCON. Expert systems have now moved well beyond these pioneering systems and a range of expert system development tools are now readily available. In particular the use of expert system shells has enabled a number of small-scale but useful expert systems to be developed in many areas of business and industry. These systems are not necessarily well reported and many may not be viewed as expert systems by some people, nevertheless they seem to be performing a useful job. A number of legal expert systems have now been developed. One large-scale project in the application of legal expert systems has been the Retirement Pension Forecast Adviser (RPFA) which is used by some

36 administrative staff at the central office of the Department of Social Security at Newcastle (Duffin, 1989). It is reported that using this expert system the 36 staff deal with 99.5 per cent of the more than 350,000 state pension forecasts which are made annually by the office. Another example is the British Nationality Act expert system which has been developed at Imperial College. Capper and Susskind have developed an expert system in the area of latent damage. This appears to be the most sophisticated example of an expert system in law to date since it combines appropriate elements of statutory laws, precedents and other legal information into the system. Thus superficially it might appear that expert systems offer the best technology yet developed for providing legal information in a manner which is usable by the lay person. However, it should be noted that to date the development of expert systems has been either so that they can act as an aid in problem solving by an expert, or so that the expertise of an individual can be moved further down the organisational hierarchy. A hypothetical example of the latter situation might be the rules used by a bank to determine whether or not a particular individual is eligible to open a particular type of bank account. The assistant at the counter might be able to deal with those customers who clearly qualify and those who clearly do not qualify given the bank's rules incorporated into an expert system. A more senior member of the bank staff will only need to be involved in the non-straightforward cases where the individual is on the borderline of acceptability to the bank and human judgement must be exercised to determine the acceptability of the person. A related example is the Bank of Ireland's Loans and Saving Advice program which has been developed to enable customers to obtain details of their credit status and what the repayments on any particular loan might be. Advice on other services is also available. This enables the more borderline cases to be dealt with by the branch manager. Thus it is reasonable to suppose that expert systems might plausibly be involved in the training of law students as suggested by Bainbridge (1989) or in the training of para-legals such as social workers or tax accountants.

## The future

Despite the considerable developments in the use of information technology in the delivery of legal information it is
noteworthy that most of the applications are in the presentation of legal information to legal and other professional
people. It is important to recognise that even in this sphere the
impact of information technology has been relatively limited
in Great Britain though there have been rather more
significant developments in the United States. Living in a
rural area, we would have expected that information
technology would have presented a means of increasing
access to legal information to the many legal professionals
who do not have ready access to primary materials. However
it is in the large City firms that the greatest developments
appear to have taken place in the use of information
technology. Information technology has hardly affected the
daily operations of legal professionals in an area such as rural
Wales. This may be partly due to the innate conservatism of
the legal profession.

In considering future developments in the application of
information technology in presenting legal information to the
general public, it must be noted that any successful application must be easy to use, readily accessible, either in the
home or in a public building, and available at a cost in time
and money that the general public will be willing to accept.
That in itself will be a tall order but it is not the whole of the
picture. It must be remembered that the most pressing need
for legal information on the part of the general public will
always be in relation to a particular problem such as conveyancing or disputes with neighbours. In these situations
what the person needs is not information but advice on how
the law applies to a specific situation. This is likely to call for
a knowledge of the legal process and how best to exploit the
law. Thus to make significant advances it will be necessary to
develop systems which go beyond the delivery of information
and to consider systems which contain all the legal
knowledge pertinent to the situation and a mechanism for
applying that knowledge in the particular situation. This
points either to the continued use of some form of intermediary, whether legal professional or advice worker, or to
the development of expert systems. The latter would seem to

hold some considerable potential but the problems should not be underestimated in an over-enthusiasm for the potential of information technology. The development of expert systems is an expensive business. Any expert system needs to be updated to take account of developments in the law. Finally, there is the difficult legal problem of accountability for the advice given to lay people by a computer system. Who is liable should the advice turn out to be inaccurate or unhelpful in a particular case?

Given these problems in the development of expert systems it is plausible that an initial application may be in use to refer people to appropriate services of information and advice. A prototype of such a system has already been developed in the sphere of gardening (see Vickery et al., 1988).

The experience with Prestel demonstrates that the public will not be impressed by a technology in search of a market, it must fulfil a real need in an acceptable manner. Thus we are led to the conclusion that significant developments in the application of information technology are most likely to occur in the delivery of legal information to legal professionals, para-professionals or advice centre workers. The use of information technology to provide direct access to the law for the general public requires considerable technological developments in the areas of intelligent systems, a greater understanding of the needs for such systems on the part of their potential users and the resolution of thorny economic and legal problems before any noteworthy developments take place. Thus we are led inexorably to the conclusions that the role of information technology in improving access to legal information is likely to be restricted in the short term to improving the access to information for legal professionals and para-professionals who can exploit that information on behalf of the public to offer an improved advice service.

Furthermore, not all areas of law lend themselves to the use of technology. Only those areas that are self-contained, logical in structure and not of a discretionary character are appropriate. Tax legislation, some social security legislation and housing legislation are suitable areas for the use of technology. Other areas, such as the law of negligence, present insurmountable problems as they are mainly creatures of case law. Also it must be recalled that proper legal advice requires an awareness of the legal environment within which it will be applied. Any advice-giving technology must, in order to be complete, take this environment into consideration. It is questionable whether technology is so advanced. Perhaps the future for technology in making law accessible to the general public lies in producing a better informed body of people who will then go better prepared to the advice giver. Information of this type will make people more aware of the legal issues that arise in their lives and enable them to approach the advice giver with a clearer idea of the legal issues involved in their problems. Thus technology is not the driving factor, rather it is the suitability of law that will dictate the pace of development. The future of technology appears to be in the provision of information to the public rather than advice.

It is important that such information is delivered to locations where it will be used by lay people and that it is presented in a manner that makes it readily usable by a wide range of people. In other words the physical and intellectual barriers to access must be removed. Thus we believe that legal information systems for lay people must be taken to the places where they will be seen and used by those people. This means that they should not be confined to libraries and other local or central government buildings but that they should be available in Post Offices, hospitals, shopping malls, pubs, hotel foyers, community centres and garden centres. This may necessitate some innovative collaboration between public and private sector but seems to be the only manner by which legal information can be brought to the public which needs it.

Another problem that will need to be considered is that of data protection. Users must be assured that any confidential information entered into a system will be secure. Access from a personal computer based in the user's home will be traceable, so it is essential that any personal information is protected. Also it cannot be assumed that use of a system will be a once-and-for-all event. It may be that personal information will have to be stored and re-accessed at a later consultation. Again it is essential for reasons of public confidence that adequate protection is given.

Clearly telecommunications technology makes the delivery of information into such a wide range of locations feasible. This physical accessibility must be complemented by intellectual accessibility. This means that the information must be presented to the users devoid of as much legal terminology as possible. In addition, the interactions at public terminals must be sufficiently straightforward and easy to use that it can be used by people with no computer experience whilst at the same time the responses are adequately rapid for those who are computer users. It seems likely that the inter-actions may best be created using such technology as touch sensitive screens, 'through the wall' videotex systems such as those sometimes seen at Tourist Information Centres. Some applications may find that it is possible to exploit the capabilities of user friendly WIMP environments such as Windows and GEM whilst others may find that hypertext systems offer acceptably straightforward user interfaces. Thus we believe that by a careful choice of the information to be presented, imaginative location of services and careful design of interfaces, it will be possible to move beyond the use of information technology for the delivery of legal infor-mation to intermediaries to the delivery of some legal infor-mation to lay people.

## References

Bainbridge, D. I. (1989) 'Expert systems and the law', *The Law Teacher*, **23**(3), pp. 279–92

Baird, P., MacMorrow, N. and Hardman, L. (1988) 'Cognitive aspects of constructing non-linear documents: Hypercard and Glasgow Online', *Online Information 88 Proceedings of the 12th Inter-national Online Information Meeting*, Oxford: Learned Infor-mation, pp. 207–18

Ball, C., Harris, R., Roberts, G. and Vernon, S. (1988) *The Law Report: Teaching and Assessment of Law in Social Work Educa-tion*, London: CCETSW Paper 4.1

Bull, G. (1986a) 'Computer assisted research' in R. Logan, *Infor-mation sources for law*, London: Butterworths, 5 pp. 337–49

Bull, G. (1986b) 'Law books for non-lawyers' in R. Logan, *Infor-mation sources in law*, London: Butterworths, 5 pp. 350–8

Department of Health (1989) *An Introduction to the Children Act 1989*, HMSO

Dover, M. (1988) 'Public Information in rural areas: technology experiment Phase 1, London: the British Library

Duffin, P. (1989) 'Expert systems in law and UK government', *Computers and Law*, no. 61, pp. 9–11

Gray, R. (1988) 'Law: British and European legal systems', in C. J. Armstrong and J. A. Large (eds), *Manual of Online search strategies*, Aldershot, Gower, pp. 507–36

Hartley, R. J. *et al.* (1990) *Online searching: principles and practice*, London, Bowker-Saur

Impey, G. (1986) 'Lawtel: the comprehensive solution', *Business Law Reviw*, **7**(4), pp. 125–6

Jones, R. P. (1989) 'Computers assisting in legal education', *The Law Teacher*, **23**(3), pp. 246–64

Logan, R. (1986) *Information sources for law*, London, Butterworths

MacMorrow, N. (1990) Personal communication

Morby, G. (1982) *Know how to find out your rights*, London, Pluto Press and Library Association Publishing

Raper, D. (1988) *Law databases 1988* London, Aslib

Sparkes, P. (1989) 'Computer-assisted legal instruction in turbo-Pascal', *The Law Teacher*, **23**(3), pp. 265–78

Wallace, J. D. (1987) 'Marketing legal services online', *Proceedings of the 8th National Online Meeting*, pp. 473–6, Medford, NJ, Learned Information

Vickery, A. *et al.* (1988) *Expert systems for referral*, London, British Library Research and Development (LIR Rep 66)

Williams, N. (1989) *Conference for contractors on artificial intelligence applications to learning programme*, Sheffield, Training Agency

# CHAPTER 3

# Community information in context: users and systems

*Patricia M. Baird,*
*Douglas Badenoch and*
*Noreen MacMorrow*

## Introduction

The concern of this chapter is one which closely resembles what Wersig characterises as being the basic aim of a problem-oriented science: that of ensuring the effective transmission of knowledge to those who need it (Wersig and Neveling (1975)). The user context which most broadly encompasses this remit is that of the community information resource.

For the most part, traditional community information comprises paper-based linear resources — pamphlets, guidebooks, directories, maps, timetables. Increasingly, however, television has been carrying 'public information' items. These televised items, and the printed sources mentioned above, have one thing in common — they do not cater for a specific user group, i.e. they do not distinguish between segments of the community; they are intended for the entire community and, in this case, that means anyone who wants to read, hear or see the message. Such information resources encompass broad categories of the user population and needs, relying on passive, mass communication for effectiveness. Users either absorb the message, sometimes act on it, or they ignore it. Alternatively, if they have a specific query they may seek out the particular information items to satisfy that need, often using the above resource types only as reference. The unique identifying characteristic of the community therefore is, paradoxically, the absence of a distinguishing mark.

Hence, users of community information resources cannot initially be characterised into straightforward functional groups. There is, in principle, no limitation on the potential user population. The 'community' cannot be assumed to have a particular, narrow interest which is to be catered for by the community information resource, unlike the conventional interest in information retrieval aimed at specific professional and functional groups. In information terms, needs and the processes of satisfying them are seldom formalised in the same way that scientific or business information needs are. Often, the presence of an intermediary is necessary to help individuals navigate the disparate resources and adapt their queries to the provisions of these resources. Thus, the community user is inhibited from information seeking by the physical and cognitive barriers imposed.

This implies that, if a useful service is to be provided, the system structure must act as the intermediary between the user and the information. The concept of system structure as intermediary introduces a new dimension into community information — interactivity. The movement is away from the user as passive recipient (in the sense of having no control over the flow of information) into active participant in the information arena. Technological developments have opened up new possibilities and provide tools for managing and disseminating vast quantities of information-offering services which allow users control over the data.

However, the service must adapt to the skills users bring to the system, present the information in such a way as to ease assimilation and yet remain flexible enough to allow users to determine the outcome of the search as far as possible. In formalised information retrieval environments, e.g. large databases using inverted file structures, the procedures to access the appropriate information are explicitly adapted to the systems available, and there is often a trade-off between allowing the user to dictate the search conditions and the development difficulties of query systems. This discussion will primarily concentrate on hypertext, a lesser known and relatively new means of information presentation, dissemination and retrieval. It will also examine and draw on the experiences of the tried and tested platform of videotex systems, which were launched in the early 1970s to meet the IT needs of the community. Videotex systems, if anything, are synonymous with the provision of community information, because the presentation medium which provides broadcast videotex — the television set — is a familiar part of modern life.

This is not to say that there is an easy 'technological fix' to the problems posed by community information retrieval. As stated above, a significant proportion of these problems are associated with the structure of the information involved in the transaction. The perceived deficiencies in the users' image-structures, which prompt them to seek out information, are heterogenous in terms of specificity, domain and urgency. Hence, this is not simply a hardware problem. It is important to realise that the form of information held within the resource will delimit its potential user population. In other words, consideration must be given to the groups within the community and their information needs in designing such resources. Consequently, a user typology in terms of cognitive, behavioural and information properties will precede a discussion of the merits and demerits of the technologies available.

## Types of users of the community information resource

In modelling a system of user requirements and likely cognitive orientation at the retrieval interface, a theoretical background is necessary to ensure consistency in the application of criteria. An elegant, simple and effective model of communication is provided by Sperber and Wilson. Briefly, this is a *productivity model* of information exchange, whereby the perceived relevance of an exchange is a result of the balance of two forces: *contextual effects* and *processing effort*. Relevance is directly proportional to the contextual effects produced by the information in the individual's image-structure, and inversely proportional to the processing effort required to access and interpret it (Sperber and Wilson, 1988). While this model implies the possibility of a quantitative assessment of the relevance and utility of a resource, such an undertaking would be dependent on the experimental manipulation of 'known' relevance values, a difficult concept to define, given that 'context' is an obscure, internal and possibly unique personal quality.

This is not to say that a subjective assessment of variables is of no value. On the contrary, it is possible to make judgements about the internal and external variables which will affect context and processing effort. Groups of users can thus be defined in these terms. A good starting-point in identifying user groups in the community is their familiarity with the community itself — ranging from lifelong residents to first-time visitors.

## Domain familiarity

The user who is seeking information in an unfamiliar community will require a wider spectrum of information than residential users with their few and predictable specific needs; hence follows the appeal of broad paper-based resources for tourist information. In many ways, this information is redundant to the familiar user, but there will be some overlap, especially in areas such as public transportation and entertainment, which could be designated as specific queries. 'Usefulness' has a much broader definition for the unfamiliar user. It corresponds to a 'utility-theoretic' retrieval context, as opposed to a strictly 'relevance-theoretic' framework, as contrasted by Regazzi. The semantic difference between 'utility' and 'relevance' in information retrieval can be seen as a difference in the completeness of the user's image-structure of the domain (Regazzi, 1988). Thus it is easier for a community information resource to be valuable to a visitor (unfamiliar user) than to a resident, as the target area of useful information is much larger and more general.

Unfortunately, it is not possible to state that users always fall into a neat category for classification. It is more likely that the same user has different degrees of familiarity with respect to different aspects of the community. Given the lack of systematic studies of the informatic processes within the community at large, a top-down approach to the modelling of user needs is appropriate.

## Behavioural orientation

Characterising familiarity in terms of specificity provides only a one-dimensional user typology. Indeed, a complex information typology may not be of use, since each user will have a multitude of information needs of varying types. Rather than pin user groups to certain information characteristics, it is suggested that a behavioural typology be applied to information retrieval. User groups can then be considered in more manageable behavioural terms.

Three types of behaviour which concern information retrieval are (Weber, 1922):

1. *Means-end* behaviour, where the individual's actions are calculated towards a consciously iterated goal. For example, searching for a university which offers a course in Information Science;
2. *Understanding* behaviour, where action is intended to elicit knowledge which will empower the individual with the ability to act if needed. For example, reading about a university's background and setting; and
3. *Ritualistic* behaviour, where action is executed without reference to a particular future goal. For example, browsing in the university library.

Judgements can be made about the information characteristics, which will be associated with users approaching the resource in these behavioural states. Means-end retrieval will tend to be well defined by the user and require high-specificity results. Business and professional information retrieval behaviour is typical of this kind of orientation, where highly specific, brief and granular information items are required, with large capacity systems which are consulted frequently.

The understanding-motivated user will have a less restrictive formulation of needs, and, hence, less specific information will also have desirable effects on the user's perception of the problem. Typical information requirements will be for references to appropriate bodies, large textual items and alternative perspectives. Ritualistic information retrieval requires low-specificity representations to engage the mind in a particular context for viewing the domain.

In the context of community information, two questions have to be posed. Firstly, should systems be designed to encompass different behavioural approaches (as described above) to the retrieval of information? If a particular user group is not rigidly defined, it will be necessary to consider such general issues in approaching their interaction with information systems. Secondly, do such systems already exist? The next step is therefore to look at the experiences of implementing public information resources.

## The videotex phenomenon

At the beginning of the seventies, videotex was heralded as the ideal information system for the inexpert or occasional user, viz., the community at large. Videotex is the general term for the retrieval of information stored on a central computer and displayed on a modified television set or a microcomputer. There are two types of videotex: broadcast videotex, or teletext, uses the spare capacity of any TV signal — frames are stored cyclically and pages are displayed one at a time. Examples of such systems in the UK are BBC's Ceefax and ITV's Oracle. Interactive videotex, or viewdata, uses a normal telephone line and a modem to link the user to the central computer. By definition, the user works interactively with the system, requesting frames of information which are displayed immediately. Users can also input information to the system.

The viewdata phenomenon is mainly a European one and, more specifically, French, Although started in the UK by the British Post Office in 1979, viewdata's perceived utility in this country has not been sufficiently evident to the general user, and therefore Prestel has never attained the success predicted. Generally, the anticipated domestic market did not materialise, except for France, where government backing and installation of the necessary hardware created the market and provided the accessing mechanism.

The major 'selling' points of videotex systems — menu-based systems and simple page displays of text and graphics — are also major weaknesses. The user-interface is unfriendly

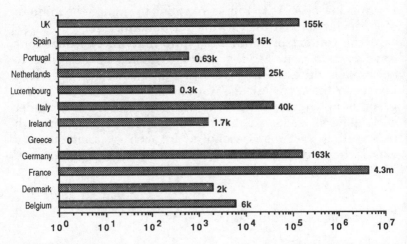

**Figure 3.1:** Number of videotex users (log scale) across the 12 EC countries in 1989

— not always intuitive; in the main, graphics are 'lego-like' and dull; page-based systems present irritating delays etc. It seems only when systems have other features integrated that their intrinsic value becomes apparent, but their user groups tend towards the homogeneous. Facilities such as gateway status and e-mail on Prestel have cemented added value and transformed the service into one which has appeal to a different user group from the original intended domestic market. Indeed, this seems to be the case in Europe in general, including France. As systems have come on stream in various countries, within a short time their predominant appeal moves in the direction of the business community.

Figures 3.1 and 3.2 show numbers of users of national videotex services across the EC in 1989, and the distribution between professional and public use. The statistics are conclusive. Videotex systems for the community at large very quickly find, post-launch, that take-up is mainly in the business market (probably for the small business user). Successful public information systems will only maintain success with the community in general if the market need is either there in the first instance, or is created and sustained. Furthermore, it is clear that the technology start-up and on-going costs must be minimal.

Community systems, however, need not always run on

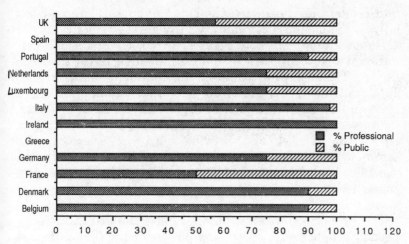

**Figure 3.2:** Professional/public distribution across the 12 EC countries in 1989

hand-outs. As of Spring 1990, five million people in France had been given Minitel sets by France Telecom. From 1981 to 1989, Télétel, the France Telecom subsidiary, invested Ffr12.3 billion to set up the system, of which Ffr6.5bn has been recouped. Revenues remain low compared to revenues generated by international database services. Yet the expected return on the initial capital in the case of the French system has materialised, with profits for France's network carriers and software/hardware suppliers; the 8,000 French information providers receive only 33 per cent of generated revenue, but this is growing. Télétel, which is a national company without capital, financed directly by generated revenues (and indirectly by taxes), is not expected, by France Telecom, to break even until well into the 1990s. But it *is* expected to break even, although not with revenue generated by the average citizenry of France.

For the average household, Minitel is too expensive. It is very easy to run up huge bills. After the brief period of *messageries roses* in the mid-1980s, this particular novelty wore thin, and the service began to gain ground as a business resource. Three-quarters of French companies have Minitel, using it for diverse purposes, such as salaries management, orders, deliveries, stock control, home shopping services, etc. The telecommunications infrastructure is already in place and Télétel traffic is increasing both at home and abroad, *but* only in the business community. An aggressive policy aimed at international markets resulted in 30,000 hours of international traffic in 1989 — more than three times the 1988 figure. Télétel's director is more confident than France Telecom. He expects the initial investment to be paid off in 1993 and an annual return of 9 per cent by 1995. It seems, therefore, that without significant public/private backing to create the market and provide hardware, viewdata for community information is destined to have only limited success. With added features, it has tapped into and capitalised on the already existing infrastructure for business users.

The French experience, however, has enabled millions of French people to use computing power for the first time and still shows 50 per cent home use, which other countries cannot ignore. During 1991, in a joint venture between IBM, Esselte and the Swedish Telecoms, SEK, it is intended to distribute 50,000 terminals to households in Sweden. The objective is to develop electronic services for home use with a projected installed base of one million in five years. The project will be called Teleguide, and has come about due to the success of the French Minitel scheme (IWR, 1990a). Similarly, the Republic of Ireland will benefit (from October 1990) from the Minitel experience, with a system based on the French videotex. The user group targeted is the home market, with terminals available by lease, at a lesser cost than monthly television rental. Services planned include home shopping and banking, travel timetables and, in a more 'value-added' arena, agricultural advice (IWR, 1990b).

## Matching systems to user need

To revert to the behavioural typology discussed above, human information-processing behaviour, in the context of community information, is primarily determined by need. Needs are varied, however, and will be conditioned by the image-structure the user has of the domain. Resident users have particular information needs, which usually pertain to highly specific, means-end retrieval. Visitors, on the other hand, have fewer means-end needs, which are therefore easier to anticipate. While both user groups may benefit from more general overview-type information, this is unlikely to be perceived need in the case of the resident. New perspectives from understanding-motivated retrieval may be of value, but residents may resent incompatibility with their own ideas in this respect.

Certain aspects of community information are frequently changing, as are the needs of user groups. This element of dynamism is closely linked to the specificity of the information, although the one does not always imply the other. In business means-end retrieval, however, where frequent consultation of resources is usual, there is only a need for the information because it may have changed since the last time it was required. Rapid updating of such resource contents is therefore essential, as is ease and speed of access. The utility of the behavioural typology is therefore linked to the degree of familiarity with the system, with the domain and also with the level of specificity required.

In summary, goal-oriented behaviour, or information seeking for a particular purpose, implies familiarity and specificity. In contrast, the case of the user seeking information for a greater understanding of the situation implies non-familiarity, but some specificity, and could be labelled background-seeking information. There are always, of course, the browsers who, by definition, search systems, whether paper-based or computerised, with no explicit aim in view. This behaviour implies no specificity but perhaps some familiarity with the domain. The cognitive disposition of the user is such that the instant impact of contextual effects must attract attention, and freedom of movement among specificity levels is paramount.

Videotex systems, on the whole, do not differentiate between types of user. Information is presented uniformly with no more than a cursory glance at the various behavioural approaches. Vast stores of what often seems to be simply decanted linear text are presented on screen with the merest hint of any over-arching structure offering multi-approach, which would acknowledge a varied group of users. Videotex, in its presentation of information, does not offer a highly differentiated product from print-based information. What it does offer is real-time information *and, perhaps more importantly*, the technical means of access which sits in the corner of the living room.

## Hypertext systems

By contrast, much hypertext research and development centres on new means of learning and communication; on exploiting the technology for what it can do for the information; on creating a value-added dimension to the information. In particular, many see hypertext becoming the norm for the handling and dissemination of public information. Ted Nelson has remarked:

> Today's conventional databases will not satisfy the information needs of the non-computing public, nor can they provide methods for publishing the ever-more interconnected writings now being placed on electronic networks. It is our hope to bring the power of electronic access to the new and sweeping literary medium of hypertext, in all the forms that the mind can devise. (Nelson, 1988)

At the moment, this is the triumph of hope over experience. For, although hypertext systems have been discussed for over forty years and various PC applications have been available for most of the eighties, there is a dearth of real systems in the public domain. There has been a burgeoning interest in hypertext and hypermedia since the late 1940s, and a sharp increase in its bibliography (Nielsen, 1989) over the past three years, in particular, since the *HyperTEXT '87* conference at North Carolina. These years have also seen an increasing number of systems become commercially available (Shneiderman and Kearsley, 1989; Baird, Davenport and MacMorrow, 1990).

So what is it? Definitions abound, from the multi-cited Vannevar Bush (Bush, 1945) through the big names in the field (Englebart, Nelson, Conklin, *et al.*) to a succinct Hardman description which is clear and comprehensible:

> The property that comes closest to defining a hypertext system is the ability to create links between items and to navigate through the hypertext using these links. (Hardman, 1990, p. 10)

Hypertext systems can facilitate storage and access capability. They go beyond the collocation of vast stores of decanted linear text, by adding value to the information; exploiting the software by repackaging the information presentation; offering a framework of connections which users can follow as they require. For novice users of such systems, however, a mental model or a pre-understanding of what the system has to offer may be under-informed. Users may not know what to expect. Only by using the system and exploring its potential does the user's mental model of the structure begin to emerge. Gaining confidence, the user can then apply a new type of information-processing behaviour to test the system against the model.

Definitions abound; interest is increasing; bibliography is growing. What does not seem to be so readily available is a growing number of significant, generally useful applications. To take just one example, it is said that currently there are over 200,000 HyperCard developments globally (Pring, 1989, pp. 19–30). It is not clear what categories the developments fall into, or even if, by virtue of scale of use, they confirm a new information paradigm. The potential is there for a paradigmatic shift in how we handle, store, access, track and share information, but whether 200,000 real (in the sense of something beyond the research stage) developments are taking place is problematic. Peter Brown (1988, 1990) identifies nine areas where problems exist, or where areas of further research are required:

1. Integration with other systems
2. Quality of authorship
3. Better tools
4. Catering for change
5. Testing and validation
6. Big systems
7. Collaborative authorship
8. Navigation
9. Cost–value–benefits

Brown points to an area of potential concern. Creative authors need to explore the unique characteristics of the medium for what it can do that is new, rather than translating the techniques of paper-based documents into hypertext systems. Is there sufficient product differentiation? Does hypertext provide a unique selling point? Is the perceived added value evident? Are the main constraints on uptake in the corporate sectors (public and private) financial, technical or political? These concerns may be among the reasons for the paucity of systems. The success or failure of future work will determine whether hypertext is the technology of the millenium or simply the technology of the moment.

The current movement is towards customised information systems, where structures do not impede functionality, nor obstruct the user who is not technically literate. Hypertext systems can be seen as personalised information environments, where there is little or no mismatch between user needs and what the system can provide.

## The hypertext public resource

Public information systems have the potential to influence considerably social communication; to provide an alternative means of access to and demystify, in some instances, the ever increasing public information arena which we need for living; and, using a hypertext platform, to wrest computing power from the élite hold and bring it to the masses. To achieve this, however, such systems must have a wide appeal, be easy to learn and provide useful, current information.

> Public information systems . . . have received little attention from researchers despite the fact that they have the potential of larger impact on society than commercial systems. They could significantly impact the social, economic and political structure of the society by changing the availability and accessibility of critical information to the general public. (Orman, 1989, pp. 69-76)

An example of a community hypertext system is *Glasgow Online*, a database of information on the City of Glasgow, which combines text, graphics, images and animation. The database integrates existing resources using Apple's Hypercard software and offers users the facility of customisable information through the traditional Macintosh interface of point and click. The research and development which led to *Glasgow Online*, and initial testing of the system, have been documented elsewhere (Baird, 1988, pp. 344-53; Baird and Percival, 1989, pp. 75-92), and the first version of the database was released in Spring 1989.

There are significant design problems for the professional

information scientist attempting to create hypertext systems for general use within the community, e.g. user-modelling within specific contexts; the temptation towards information overload; cognitive activity of heterogeneous user groups; orientation problems and recovery measures in a non-linear, non-sequential information environment. These problems can only be addressed within an extended period of testing both during development and in use. The testing done on *Glasgow Online* (Baird and Percival, 1989, pp. 75–92; Hardman, 1989, pp. 34–63) indicates, on the whole, that users do get the information they require and enjoy the experience of using the system.

To extrapolate from the experiences of the Glasgow database, hypertext systems offer a friendly user interface which is appealing to end-users, especially novice users, with in-built recovery procedures in the event of the user becoming lost in the hyperdocument. It has the advantage over traditional community information systems, which are often presented in videotex format and which do not offer the same degree of user control. In addition, the user interface in the Macintosh environment, offering features such as pull-down menus and help windows, provides an incomparably friendlier interface than screens full of structured information. The interactivity of the videotex database, e.g. British Telecom's Prestel or the BBC's Ceefax, is largely determined by the tree and branch structure of the system. Users can call up pages of information as required, but are often frustrated by being locked into a sub-set of the data. Once in the system, the user loses full control. The system determines direction of the data, speed of access, when the user can exit and seldom offers backtracking facilities. Browsing is, of course, possible, but only so far as the system structure will permit. Hypertext, by contrast, offers the user an information resource in which the technology, to use Englebart's dictum, should augment the information, rather than the reverse.

The 'text' in a hypertext does not exist as a formally delineated structure: each reader creates his own text from the corpus of available material, choosing routes and adding links in the process. Dynamic hypertexts are thus read — and write — systems. Hypertext creation blurs the distinction between recipient and sender, making the direction of communication less one-sided. Both author and user have to consider the nature of the information structure, and how and under what conditions it will be accessed and retrieved. By definition, in dynamic hypertexts, the structure of the information is not fixed.

Allowing open structuring of links in different contexts and with different users implies a continuing metamorphosis of the hypertext, which will perhaps threaten the usability of the original. The loss of the impact of low-specificity, high-level information as represented in links is a real danger where large numbers of authors are contributing to the same hyper-document. Some system of masking or filtering conditional links is necessary, so that the information may be viewed without affecting the integrity of the original hyperdocument, or there is no definitive document. Alternatively, if we have no problems with losing the original form, links should be classified according to retrieval context in order to maintain the value of high-level structure. It would seem, therefore, in a wider information-rich environment, that cognitive models of writing and reading will have to change.

The question of allowing the public full read/write privileges in such systems is doubtful, as much 'junk' would inevitably be introduced, unless such creations were perso-nalised and kept apart from the main system. The creation of such systems, therefore, relies on a centralised research effort to produce core hyperdocuments. Unfortunately, public infor-mation systems often lack the commercial backing, market-ing procedures and technical development which is common to private or internal systems. Because of the unformalised nature of community information needs, it is difficult to justify the investment of public money into developing sys-tems, as utility cannot be guaranteed and need cannot be proven.

## Behavioural disposition in hypertext information retrieval

As previously stated, business (professional) information needs are highly specific, dynamic and well formalised in most cases, and, hence, are often dealt with internally. Infor-mation about the community, which is needed by such users, will be similar in nature — information about quality of accommodation for clients; the range, price and quality of services available from contractors, etc. The specialist nature of the business will dictate the individual context for information retrieval, but such a context will tend to be strictly goal-oriented, means-end behaviour according to Weber's analysis.

This sort of query demands less fine-tuning as the user progresses towards the goal. The necessity on the part of the user to make decisions at low-specificity levels as to which branch of the domain hierarchy contains the required information may hinder the process, as this introduces the potentially misleading incongruence of the personal image-structure with the system's structure, imposing additional processing effort on the user.

The less formalised information retrieval habits of the general population imply that they lack a rigid, low-specificity frame of reference defining separate branches of the domain: the low-specificity context for retrieval is less dynamic. Hence, the low-specificity ordering of the domain within the hypertext community information resource will be more useful and less prone to incongruence effects. The non-business user, however, has more variable behavioural orientations. The sub-domain concerned, and the user's familiarity with it, will determine the type of behaviour manifest. Again, high familiarity implies high specificity, if any information is required at all.

### Residential users

Having stated that the tendency of such users' needs will be for specific information, this does not mean that the user will necessarily know how to satisfy a particular need. Indeed, this is often the major information problem facing such people. In particular, people who are unaccustomed to the systematic manipulation and retrieval of information for a specific purpose often encounter difficulty when they are required to interact with institutions — especially the legal establishment and the social security system — which demand they conduct their interaction in terms of particular information items. These are items which are usually designed to ease the institution's internal machinations, rather than permit user-friendly relations with the individual.

The easiest way to ameliorate this problem is for the user to adapt the query to the needs of the organisation. Indeed, this is inevitable given the size of these institutions and their need for efficiency. The combination of the user's unfamiliarity with the informatic nature of the organisation and the refusal of the organisation to accept any communication which is incompatible with its informatic processes lies at the root of many problems which exist in the relationship between individuals and organisations, causing frustration, anger and sometimes even violence.

Such problems are best seen as concerning cognitive conceptual structure. Detailed information items cannot be exchanged, not because of any absence of crucial items, but because the low-specificity arrangements of these items in the respective participants are incompatible. The individual interacting with the system has little understanding of the context in which the system views him, and vice versa. Communication breakdown is seen as a result of these higher-level processes. The information resources which conduct this exchange should bear the responsibility for failure, as they cannot establish equivalence relations between two alien frames of reference.

Other societal informatic phenomena can be seen in a similar light. For example, it is a common fallacy that most citizens have few real information needs regarding the community in which they live. The evidence for such views arises not out of a general apathetic malaise, but rather from the presence of significant barriers between the citizen and the achievement of the level of understanding which would enable more considered approaches to the issues affecting the community (Lamont, 1975, pp. 553–61). The behavioural incongruity of seeking out understanding-related information, while having to possess a determination more akin to means-end retrieval in accessing the resources, mitigates against the development of such an understanding.

Hypertext's design flexibility can be used to structure the information required of the individual into a conceptual scheme which reflects the user's level of understanding. For example, prospective income-support claimants can be directed towards nodes which indicate the information they must supply to the DHSS, with cross-links showing how these are related to other benefits available to them, and how and why the DHSS uses this information in validating their claims. In this way, the interaction between the individual and the organisation is lubricated, and a greater understanding of the internal operations of such organisations engendered in the individual.

## Cost

The cost of producing the system — or rather, how its availability is limited by cost — is a very important consideration here. Certain information resources, such as telephone directories, cost little to make and therefore can be distributed to each telephone. (It is ironic however, that, by computerising the telephone directory, France Telecom created the initial thrust for Minitel traffic and saved Ffr217 million on telephone books and Ffr300 million on the telephone enquiries service between 1984 and 1989.) The more expensive the system is to produce and run, the fewer can be made available per head of population. This means that the user will tend to consult the resource as a result of a perceived need for information, rather than out of casual interest, as is often the case in public access points like libraries. If access points are relatively few, the user will have limited time to investigate the information. Exploration to enhance understanding and ritualistic browsing will be inhibited, and efficiency of search will become paramount. Cognitive dissonance may inhibit retrieval performance where the user is pressurised by, for example, an impatient queue of would-be users. Hypertext, at some cost, can structure the information in such a way as to facilitate efficient access, and the effectiveness of this structuring must be addressed in an assessment of the resource as a whole. Cost also must be addressed.

## Costs versus perceived benefits

Research and development into computerised systems points up the inadequacy of some paper-based systems for the purposes of information retrieval. Hypertext developments can provide some solutions, but at some expense. Development time can be extremely labour intensive even with a

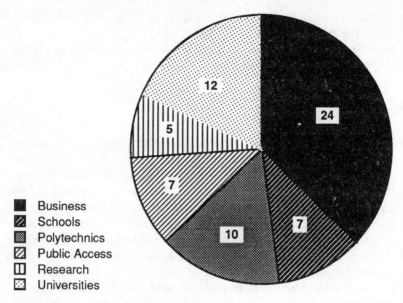

**Business**
**Schools**
**Polytechnics**
**Public Access**
**Research**
**Universities**

**Figure 3.3:** Glasgow Online sites

supportive package like Hypercard, which removes some of the fundamental design effort. The intellectual content is significant, labour costs are high and are not likely to diminish if the finished product is to be perceived as a value-added item.

The *Glasgow Online* project took 16 man-years to produce a 16Mb database, though almost 50 per cent was learning-curve time, since the project start coincided with the release of Hypercard in Europe in late 1987. Total costs amounted to £170,000, and, although tangible benefits are difficult to quantify in a public domain information system, it can be said that the *Glasgow Online* system provides an integrated information system which offers significantly different features from traditional printed information, both in breadth of information but, more especially, in the flexibility which the medium offers. However, although potential sites have been arising daily since the database was launched, many steer clear when they realise the capital investment involved to get the system up and running. Over sixty sites now have *Glasgow Online*, but as Figure 3.3 shows, a minority are in the public domain.

## Processing effort

However, there are not only barriers of availability and cost: the resources exist in public and specialist libraries whereby virtually any information need can be satisfied. Two factors mitigate most heavily against the pursuit of such knowledge: firstly, the user's unfamiliarity with the informatic nature of the domain prevents an effective formulation of the query and, secondly, the effort involved (both cognitive in continually refining query forms and integrating information found, and physical in accessing and searching) discourages the individual from setting out on such a course in the first place. The contextual effects of the information retrieved are likely to be minimal in the initial stages, and certainly insufficient to provide an acceptable reward for the time and effort expended. Viewed in this light, the popularity of the glib, truncated homilies of tabloid journalism emerges as a natural response to the imbalance of processing effort over contextual effects.

By presenting very general information in an explicit and user-friendly manner, hypertext systems have the capability of guiding such relatively casual users towards more specific details. Undefined interests are honed towards information with the minimum of processing effort. Since this user has, by definition, low familiarity with such a domain, the contextual effects of information so retrieved are likely to be more profound and surprising than with the familiar user. Users can thus be aided in defining their interests within the community and encouraged to take an interest in the issues affecting it.

## Ideology of information

Of course, this notion invites the question of who decides what information goes into the system. The more abstract the information becomes, the more it is subject to ideological distortion and control. More general information is, by definition, more subjective and less easy to test than specific items. In a community resource, the elimination of alternative perspectives on a problem could prejudice the user towards a particular course of action. Similarly, the inclusion of certain services — or even the order of presentation of alternatives (a problem particularly relevant to hypertext) — can be seen as prejudicial.

It is obviously impossible to be completely impartial in the structuring of the community information resource. Much of its value in a hypertext system derives from the very imposition of an ideological structure to protect the user from a deluge of largely useless information (Doland, 1989, pp. 6–19). The designers of such resources should, however, be aware of the potential for the tacit manipulation of users — especially visitors to the community — and should guard against this. The precise effects of, and potential for, such manipulation is an area of information retrieval which would benefit from systematic study and measurement.

## References

Baird, P. (1988) 'Hypercard opens an electronic window on Glasgow', *The Electronic Library*, 6, no. 5, October, pp. 344–53

Baird, P., Davenport, L. and MacMorrow, N. (1990) 'Hypertext and hypermedia: the transformation of text', *Library and Information Briefings*, no. 19, British Library Board

Baird, P. and Percival, M. (1989) 'Glasgow Online: database development using Apple's Hypercard', *Hypertext: theory into practice*, Blackwell Scientific Publications, pp. 75–92

Brown, P. (1988) 'Hypertext: the way forward' in van Vleit (ed.), *Documentation manipulation and typography*, Cambridge University Press

Brown, P. (1990) 'Hypertext: dreams and reality' in Proceedings of the conference at Brunel University, *Hypertext/hypermedia and object-oriented databases*, Chapman Hall (in press)

Bush, V. (1945) 'As we may think', *Atlantic Monthly,* **176**, July pp. 101–8

Doland, V. M. (1989) 'Hypermedia as an interpretive act', *Hypermedia*, **1**(1), pp. 6–19

Hardman, L. (1989) 'Evaluating the usability of the Glasgow Online hypertext', *Hypermedia*, **1**(1), pp. 34–63

Hardman, L. (1990) 'Hypertext 89: two years on from Hypertext 87?', *IT News: new technologies and learning in Europe,* no. 2, March, p. 10

IWR (1990a) *Information World Review*, no. 49, May/June, Learned Information, Oxford

IWR (1990b) *Information World Review*, no. 50, July/August, Learned Information, Oxford

Lamont, V. C. (1975) 'Computer-based communications media and citizen participation' in A. Debons and W. J. Cameron (eds.),

*Perspectives in Information Science*, Noordhoff, Leyden, pp. 553–61

Nelson, T. H. (1988) 'Managing immense storage', *BYTE*, **13**(1), pp. 225–38

Nielsen, J. (1989) 'Hypertext bibliography', *Hypermedia,* **1**(1), pp. 74–91

Orman, L. V. (1989) 'Public information systems', *The Information Society,* **6**(1/2), pp. 69–76

Pring, I. (1989) 'Survey: interactive multimedia', *Information User*, March/April, pp. 19–30

Regazzi, J. J. (1988) 'Performance measures for information retrieval systems — an experimental approach', *Journal of the American Society for Information Science,* **39**(4), pp. 235–51

Shneiderman, B. and Kearsley, G. (1989) *Hypertext hands-on! — an introduction to a new way of organizing and accessing information*, Addison-Wesley

Sperber, D. and Neveling, U. (1975) 'The phenomena of interest to information science', *The Information Scientist,* **9**(4), pp. 127–40

Weber, M. (1922) *Wirtschaft and Gesellschaft*, 1st edn., Tubingen, translated by A. M. Henderson and T. Parsons, *The Theory of Social and Economic Organisation*, The Free Press, Glencoe (1957)

Wersig, G. and Neveling, U. (1975) 'The phenomena of interest to information science', *The Information Scientist,* **9**(4), pp. 127–40

# CHAPTER 4

# The provision of immediate community information on local radio

*Anne Martin and
Bob Usherwood*

## Introduction

Spend fifteen minutes or so touring the AM and FM dials on the average radio set and you will become party to a great deal of what information professionals term, 'community information'. One such tour in the Sheffield area produced, in just quarter of an hour, the following types of information: summer holiday events for children, debt advice, what to do after A levels, how to set up a special event radio station, job vacancies, what to do in the event of a road accident, consumer protection information and the tide times at Skegness. All that was in addition to the regular road, weather and other information slots that are the subject of the paper that follows.

Most of this information came from the BBC talk-based local radio stations, and it is true that there must be some question over their future development given the continuing pressure on, and the government's dislike of, the licence fee. In addition, significant changes in British radio are likely to take place as a result of the recent Broadcasting Bill. However, unlike the changes in television, these have scarcely been debated. Yet as a result of this bill, commercial radio will have no, or little, public service obligation, and there can be little doubt that the future development of commercial radio will mean less high quality speech and less local information as market pressures come to bear. Indeed, one of the more recent trends is for commercial stations, including some BBC stations, to group together for significant parts of the day, producing, at best, regional, rather than local programmes.

Some local information is also provided by the pirate, often ethnic-based stations. The bill does say some encouraging things about the development of community radio, but it must remain doubtful if small community groups, with even smaller budgets, will be able to survive in the thrusting entrepreneurial world of commercial radio envisaged by the British government.

At a recent Amarc World Conference, hosted by the National Association of Community Broadcasters, 400 delegates from four continents spoke of the trials and tribulations of community broadcasting world-wide. 'Amarc, financed by UNESCO and various relief agencies, does not disguise its objective of encouraging radio under popular control as a weapon of economic and social liberation' (Connolly, 1990). The precise form that this takes varies from country to country. In India, for example, radio has played an important part in the development of literacy, whilst in South Africa, the ANC-controlled Radio Freedom has broadcast from Lusaka in an attempt to overcome government powers to suppress information.

In the less-developed world, radio is likely to be the most available and accessible technology for some time to come. In this country, the future of public service broadcasting is less clear. One recent publication (Lewis and Booth, 1990) has suggested that a way forward might be to develop community radio along the lines of Channel Four, but perhaps the most apt comment has come from Peter Fiddick who has said, 'Frankly, all you can say with safety about the future of radio in this country is "it all depends" ' (Fiddick, 1987).

## Introduction to project

This chapter is based on a research project that was carried out in the summer of 1988 to evaluate one form of community information; 'information slots', provided by the English local radio station, BBC Radio Sheffield (Martin, 1988). The actual data collected will not be analysed in great detail here, but the survey results will be used to help the discussion of what should be taken into account when creating an information slot.

Information slots are one of the forms in which community information is broadcast by local radio, and until now they have been somewhat of a poor relation in the media-studies field. The broadcasting of community information can be broadly separated into two distinct categories — features and information slots. Features include interviews in the studio, outside broadcasts at important local events and reports. These tend to be relatively long items dealing with news and newsworthy items of information — for example, women's health or race relations — and often one of their predominant features is that they are used to assess information; to discuss the qualitative aspects of the information content. In other words, the information provided can be questioned and debated. 'Information slot' is a term used for the second form of information broadcast; it refers to the small items of information that are of immediate use to the listeners. These are short items, usually only a few seconds long, broadcast on a regular basis. The information that is broadcast in this way tends to be information that needs to be regularly updated and is only for use for a short period of time, often only a few hours. These information slots consist of the basic facts: the actual content of the information is not discussed and not questioned. The weather news that is broadcast on the majority of radio stations falls into this latter category, as does the travel and traffic news.

During the period in which the research for the project was carried out, six main forms of information slot were presented on Radio Sheffield — the travel and traffic news; weather news; local events information; lost pets; gas/electricity meter rotas; time announcements; and radio-frequency announcements. Two other forms of information slot were also broadcast at appropriate times of the year, the snow line and the pollen count. The snow line was broadcast during severe winter weather conditions and the pollen count was announced during the high pollen summer months. The only slots that there appeared to be on the national stations were the weather and travel news. In general, there tend to be more kinds of information slot broadcast on the local radio stations than on the national stations. This is because the local stations have a well-defined community with particular information needs; for example, local stations often broadcast a slot with information about local events which would be of use only to that community. Indeed, the BBC research department had identified radio as being the most commonly chosen primary source for accessing travel information; and most listeners named a local station as their first choice of radio station for obtaining travel news. Information slots are made up of information that may be of immediate relevance to the public and is important to them in their daily lives. The information is also continually changing. These characteristics mean that they are ideally suited for broadcasting information in extreme conditions and emergencies, and during severe weather conditions or times when the traffic situation is particularly bad. The public tends to turn to the radio, particularly the local radio, for just this type of information.

The content of the broadcasts, that is the information presented, and the style of the broadcast, that is the presentation of the information, are very different for information features and information slots. However, although both categories are distinct, there can sometimes be a connection between them, as occasionally the information announced in the information slot can be the basis for a longer, more evaluative item which is broadcast as a feature. An example would be a warning of extremely cold conditions, resulting in an item on the problems of the cold for the elderly.

The actual term 'information slot' was assigned following an examination of the literature and discussion with broadcasting and information experts. This showed that there did not appear to be any definition of, or term used for, this form of information. The term was given because the information was brief and easily distinguishable from the rest of the programme within which it is announced. It tends to be slotted in between the other items, music, interviews and features.

The project on which this chapter is based was concerned with evaluating the information, in particular the community information, that is broadcast on local radio, and it concentrated on the information slots broadcast by BBC Radio Sheffield. The study was concerned with whether the information that the station broadcast was of relevance to the audience, whether it was what the audience wanted and whether it was presented in a suitable form. The main emphasis of the project was a survey of the public's perceptions of the information slots that are broadcast on the radio, with special emphasis on the slots on local radio stations. The aim was to obtain an initial impression about how the slots were perceived by the public and to give some ideas on possible improvements and alterations.

## Methodology

In order to develop an effective survey, a thorough examination of the literature was carried out to see if anything like this had been done before. This literature search provided an interesting insight into what have been the predominant interests of the media researchers in the past. The history and development of public service broadcasting proved to be one of the much covered areas, particularly that of the British Broadcasting Corporation, the world leader in the area of public service broadcasting (Francis, 1985, and Green, 1960). In 1981 the Volunteer Centre undertook a study of advice giving through local radio (Volunteer Centre Media Project, 1982), but, in general, relatively little attention has been given to the history and development of the immediate information, the information slot, aspect of the broadcasting. There is also a considerably greater emphasis on national broadcasting services, rather than on the smaller, local and community services. The majority of the information that was available on the local and community stations referred to the consultative document on the future of radio. This allowed for a greater number of franchises for radio stations, and that was particularly aimed at setting up independent local stations, although it did recognise the public service role of the BBC local radio service (Home Office, 1987).

The actual research methodology for assessing and evaluating local radio was covered in the literature, but again did not specifically refer to the information slot form of broadcast. Several items included investigations into the problems of how to measure and classify radio audiences, and how to discover how well the information broadcast is received. Most of this research has concentrated on the commercial stations in the United States of America (Nemiroff and Linke, 1982), although the European Society of Opinion and Market Research has had many discussions on the research problems that are inherent in the field of broadcasting (European Society Opinion Market Research, 1984). The language that is used in broadcasting has been the subject of much academic research, as has the relationship between language in broadcasting and the social and political relationships of the contributors (Volunteer Centre Media Project, 1980).

The only instances of articles referring directly to the information in which the project was interested were in newspapers. In particular, the newspapers covered the presentation of the weather forecasts as there have been many developments in the television broadcasting of the weather news, particularly with the new satellite facilities and increased use of computer graphics. One particularly interesting and amusing instance was found in *The Times* in 1985 (Young 1985) which was an article concerned with how Radio York offered air time 'to those who believe their aches and pains, fits of depression, or changes of behaviour, forecast the weather more accurately than the meteorological office'. The dearth of articles and reports about the subject of information slots, and the general avoidance of this subject in the major texts, led to the conclusion that the project was covering a new area of study, and that this form of information had not been recognised as of major importance by either the academic community, or the press.

In order to gain a thorough insight into the construction, presentation, importance and relevance of the information slots, an analysis was carried out of the slots broadcast on various radio stations. This analysis was dissimilar from a comprehensive content analysis in that only the quantitative factors were examined and the qualitative factors of the content were ignored. Also the relationship of the slots to the rest of the broadcast was not examined. Seven stations were recorded between 7 and 9 am on weekdays, a time when Radio Sheffield broadcasts the greatest number of information slots.

The main method of data collection for the survey was street interviews with the public, with the analysis of the radio broadcasts being used to help in the construction of the survey questions. The interview schedule developed was structured and similar to that of the questionnaire. This has the advantage that responses can be compared, as the questions are asked in a precise way and in a precise order, and therefore the interviewees are reacting to the same stimulus. This technique was used for the majority of the schedule; however, in various places the technique was altered in order to elicit an unstructured response to allow the interviewees to respond in their own terms and thus expound on their own views. The technique that was used in this instance was that of the standardised open-ended interview. All questions were designed to make the respondents use their own words, and not to lead them (Stone, 1984). The survey had four major elements. The first section was concerned with the specific listening habits of the interviewee, in order to obtain a general context in which to assess the views of the respondent. The second section was designed to extract the respondents' opinions concerning the information slots that they had heard. A rating system was used with this section of the schedule in order for the respondents to evaluate their opinions of certain aspects; however, many of the respondents also answered with words and these were also recorded. The third section dealt with an extremely brief, but integral part of the radio broadcasting — the time and radio-frequency announcements — and the final section was to extract the personal demographic details of the respondent. The public interviews, of which there were sixty-seven, were carried out over three weeks in July 1988. Three locations were used — central Sheffield, a new shopping and leisure centre on the southern edge of the city and a village in Derbyshire. Each interview took between 10 and 15 minutes, and either one or two information slots were covered by each respondent.

Apart from the street interviews, six members of the BBC radio Sheffield Local Radio Advisory Council were also interviewed. Local Radio Advisory Council members are appointed by the BBC Board of Governors to represent the public to the station management. They are appointed to the Council for a limited period of time, so as to ensure that new opinions, ideas and interests are continually communicated to the station management (Radio Sheffield):

> The Local Radio Advisory Council meets regularly to advise the managers of Radio Sheffield on programme content and present future programme policy. The council relies on listeners to contact it with comments, concerns, proposals about what they hear on Radio Sheffield. The council also has three specialist sub-committees to consider religious and education programmes and broadcasting for minority ethnic groups and here it is assisted by advisers selected from local interest groups.

It was felt that, by interviewing members of this council, a more in-depth public view might be extracted. However one of the interesting outcomes of the survey was, in fact, the differences that appeared between the general public responses and that of the council members, which illustrates how hard it is ever to get true representatives of public opinion. The six interviews were based on the public survey schedule, but the interviewees this time answered questions on all information slots that they had heard, rather than just one or two. Each of these interviews also attempted to derive more generalised comments and views about the role of Radio Sheffield within the community, with special regard to the immediate information services. All of the presenters on Radio Sheffield were also interviewed, again following a schedule based on the public survey. It had been the original intention to compare the views of the presenters with that of the public's; however, the restrictions on time and resources made this an impossibility, and it is hoped that this element of the research can be carried out at some other time.

## Information collection

The development of an information slot for a radio broadcast consists of three major actions — collecting the information, deciding what information to broadcast and presenting the information. The first action, that of collecting the information together, will vary with the type of radio station and information slot that is required. The information can be obtained from numerous sources, including interested organisations, such as the local police force for local traffic conditions, the public, word of mouth, local newspapers and so on. There are two major forms that this collection can take — reactive or proactive. In general, the radio stations tend to be rather more reactive than proactive, relying far more on having the information brought to their attention than actively seeking the information out, though this does depend on the actual information slot itself. For example, the information for the lost pets slot on Radio Sheffield came exclusively from the public who wrote or rang in with their information. The station never actively went out to search for this information. The local events 'What's on diary' was similar, except, in this case, the station did have forms which were left at the local public library and the studio in the centre of town. However, this still meant that it was up to the public to inform the station of the local events. This dependence on the public can mean that certain areas of information are neglected and others may predominate, which, in turn, will mean that the information slot does not take on the importance that it should within the broadcast.

There are various reasons for this inactive gathering of information, the main one being the lack of resources. The actual quantity of the possible information is also a serious problem. As the programme manager for Radio Sheffield said, there was enough information about local events to fill an entire day's broadcast. It would appear that the less substantial information slots, the ones that tend to be only on the local station rather than the national stations, are based on information that is gathered in this reactive way. At the same time, radio stations tend to be more proactive in collecting the information for the other, more substantial information slots, such as the weather news and traffic bulletins. For example, the Radio Sheffield travel bulletin is made up of two different types of information: firstly, the major road news that came directly from the South Yorkshire Police, which tended to be more reactive than proactive, and, secondly, information on the local public transport services. In this latter case, the station was definitely proactive, in that it was the job of a programme assistant to keep in regular contact with the local bus companies, British Rail and the local airports throughout the day. It would appear that the importance that a station places on an information slot, not surprisingly, affects the method of collection of information for that slot. If a slot can be made to be more important to a radio station, then the information gathering and, therefore, the success of that slot, may be improved. One possibility is for the radio station to work in close collaboration with other organisations that may be able to utilise the information, such as the local library or newspaper. For example, the information that Radio Sheffield acquires for the local events slot is made up into a diary for the presenters to use in their broadcasts, and this could be placed in the local library for the public to browse through. This service would have the added benefit of publicising the information slot and radio station to a wider section of the public, therefore increasing the information gathering net. The added publicity might also help in releasing more resources for some form of proactive information collection.

## Information content

The second action that is required in creating an information slot is that of deciding what information should be broadcast. There are many criteria that can be taken into consideration: those that predominate will depend on the specific radio station concerned. The main point to be made is that the information should be relevant to the listener. The survey found that, overall, the public thinks that the information broadcast in this way on the radio network is relevant to their needs. In order to make the information relevant to the listener, several points need to be considered. The local conditions of the radio area must be taken into account. These will include social, economic, political and physical characteristics. For example, the survey found that the weather news was the most important information slot for people in the Sheffield area. This can be explained by the physical location of Sheffield on the edge of the Yorkshire dales, situated between five hills, so that the area is prone to severe weather changes. The social and economic conditions that need to be considered will include such things as the public transport system. For example, the survey found that a great many of the people in Sheffield area are as much concerned with public transport information as with general road conditions. This is not surprising as only 52 per cent (from the 1981 census) owned their own car, and also Sheffield was renowned, prior to bus deregulation and the abolition of the metropolitan counties, for its low public transport fares. Indeed, the information needs to be tailored towards the people of the local area. It would be of no use to either the radio station, or to the public, if, for example, the local events information consisted of events far out of reach of the local community in both location and price. The information needs to be targeted at an audience, and the public survey found that the information broadcast in the information slots across the various radio stations was most useful to those in the age range from 25 to 54. However, this age range does not necessarily fit the age range of a radio station audience.

One of the problems radio stations often have, partly because of their constitution, is that they are attempting to reach everyone in a community. One of the founding conditions of BBC local radio stations is that they should attempt to reach everyone in that local community, however disparate the members of that community must be. This can mean that a decision has to be taken whether to make all of the information slightly relevant to all of the community all of the time, or whether to target specific groups. The area over which the station broadcasts is another aspect that must be taken into consideration. This is particularly true when the boundaries between local and national radio are taken into consideration. Indeed, the survey found that many people considered that the national stations, in particular Radio One, were, in effect, acting as local stations for the London and South-East England area with their information slots. The comment from one respondent was that the weather news on Radio One 'just concentrates on London'. Also the survey showed that a proportion of the public wanted information about non-local events on the local radio, or wanted local events on the national radio, with quotations emerging such as 'need to combine national and local news' and 'needs more world/continental weather'. One of the problems that the public survey identified, and that was not really understood by the radio station personnel, was that of switching channels on the radio. Unless they used a preset radio, many of the public had problems switching channels. This can mean that, although relevant information is broadcast somewhere on the radio network, the problems of finding it can put the public off, thus resulting in them wanting a full information output with both national and local information on the one station.

Another aspect of the information slot that needs to be taken into consideration is that often the slot is of interest to more than one audience and this may not be foreseen. For example, the survey found that the pollen count was of interest not just to those who suffer from hay fever, but also to the family and friends of the sufferers. Indeed, one respondent stated that 'it might be useful for employers to find out why their staff are miserable'. Another case was that of the gas and electricity meter rotas broadcast on Radio Sheffield, when the lists of street places were important to the public because of their innate localness: the public just like to hear the local places being read out and identified. As one interviewee said 'I imagine the places I know with the meter readers going round. And the places I don't know, and I just wonder where they are'.

As well as the same information being of use to different audiences, one must be aware of the problems of including more than one form of information of interest to different audiences within the same slot. For example, the Radio Sheffield travel and traffic news bulletins attempted to cover both road and public transport information. There proved to be two distinctly different audiences for this slot, those driving through the area on the major motorways, and those local people in the area needing both the public transport and the local road conditions. This problem was compounded by the fact that Radio Sheffield was involved in an experiment, in cooperation with the Department of Transport, the Automobile Association and the Royal Automobile Club, to publicise the travel news to the motorway traffic. The area over which Radio Sheffield broadcasts has a number of major motorways running through it, the main one being the M1 running North and South. In return for the motorist organisations paying for motorway signs which advertised the radio frequencies of both Radio Hallam and Radio Sheffield, the stations had to provide a traffic bulletin, which would be relevant to the motorway traffic, every half hour. The station had also made great attempts to include other road information and information on the public transport system. However, the public survey found that, of those who talked about this form of information on Radio Sheffield, the majority said that it was only of use to those with their own transport. One of the problems was that the information about the motorway conditions tended to be of a more long-term nature, and also the information was easy to obtain. Indeed, information about the other transport systems tended to be broadcast only during the early morning. Also the fact that the station had to slant the information towards the motorway traffic meant that this audience was the one most targeted. In this case, it might have been more effective to ensure that the information was more split up, and perhaps broadcast as two different slots.

Another criterion that needs to be taken into account when dealing with information slots is that of defining the boundaries between them. The public survey found that the public is often interested in combined information from different slots. For example, they expressed a need for details about travel conditions to be combined with the local events information, and with details of how the weather forecast would affect travel conditions, such as black ice. The survey also found that the public often wanted more subjective, chatty information to be included with the brief factual information. For example, it was suggested that remedies for hay fever should be given along with the pollen count. However, including this sort of information directly in the information slot would fundamentally alter the nature of the slot and, indeed, might make the information appear less factual and, therefore, less accurate to the rest of the audience. There are possibilities, however, of, for example, announcing the factual information of where to find the more subjective information, or for bringing such information up later in the same programme, but distinctly separated from the information slot.

The actual information that is included in an information slot does not have to be particularly important for the majority of the listeners in order for it to be appreciated. For example, the lost pets information slots on the local radio just consist of details about specific pets, and is of no use to the vast majority of the listeners. However, it does play an important part in making the local radio appear local and accessible to the community.

A particularly good example of local radio being accessible to the community is to be found in Radio Sheffield's relationship with Community Access Radio (CAR). CAR was established in response to requests from the local voluntary sector for greater access to local radio. It started in Sheffield in April 1988 under the auspices of what was then the Sheffield Council for Voluntary Service (now Voluntary Action Sheffield). It has a steering group which reflects many of the community information interests in the city, including the City Library, BBC Radio Sheffield, the Polytechnic's Communication Studies Department and the University's Department of Information Studies.

The aims of the project were, and are, to help local community and voluntary groups publicise their needs 'on air', raise public awareness of community issues and assist in the development of new groups. CAR is a voluntary organisation relying on a part-time project coordinator and volunteers, who receive training in basic radio skills, to maintain its service. It is independent of local radio, although the studio from which it now broadcasts was built for it by BBC Radio Sheffield. In its initial stage, the project operated from a basement in Sheffield City Libraries' Manor Community Library.

Since it was set up, CAR has established a regular 'Helpline' feature on Radio Sheffield's morning programme, and has also sought to increase the public visibility of the voluntary sector through the use of public service announcements. These PSAs are recorded with the help of the CAR team, who also provide advice on the script. Once recorded the PSAs are transferred to cartridges and put in the studio at Radio Sheffield, where they are played at the discretion of presenters. They thus reach a much larger audience than would be the case with a single interview or Helpline slot.

The Helpline is broadcast at 9.45 am each weekday morning, and provides an opportunity for local community, voluntary and statutory organisations to appeal directly to the local community for help. This can be for help in finding volunteers, or items, for the clients of voluntary groups, or equipment for groups. Events can also be advertised as part of the Helpline. A Helpline 'update' is broadcast later in the morning, at around 12.20 pm, which enables CAR to thank people who have helped or responded and/or ask again for help.

It is a condition of the Helpline slot that the request for help should be on behalf of the organisations, and not directly for individuals. The messages broadcast in the slot cannot be appeals for funds, nor should they be of such a kind that they could be interpreted as giving support for a particular political party or religious viewpoint. The most usual type of requests are from organisations looking for house furniture and equipment on behalf of their clients: beds, fridges, chairs, the kind of things most of us take for granted. However, the project has also been successful in satisfying more unusual requests. These have included requests for an exterminator for a wasps' nest, a large pumpkin for a Hallowe'en disco, bat food, portable toilets, a tree costume and a bowl of goose grease. The latter, which was satisfied three times over, was required on behalf of someone who was suffering from chest pains. Each day's Helpline will deal with about thirty calls requesting or offering help. In addition, the project receives a number of calls not directly related to the broadcast, seeking help or advice.

This kind of partnership between local radio, voluntary organisations and public bodies is now becoming more common. In addition to the Sheffield CAR, mention should also be made of the successful project run by Nottingham CVS.

The information that is broadcast as an information slot can also be important in presenting the station's credibility. For example, if a station states that it is a local community radio station, then the fact that the information is of use only to that community will give the station greater credibility. One example of this is Radio Sheffield's gas and electricity meter rotas, which the public greatly appreciated. However, the stations do need to be careful not to waste time broadcasting information in a way that is of no use to the public. For example, the survey found that 54 per cent of the public did not find the radio-frequency announcements useful as the public could not understand the information, or could not catch it, and needed it written down. In this case, the slots appeared to be more of an advertisement for the stations than useful information. Indeed, the name of the station without the frequency details would have been sufficient.

Information in the wrong hands can be a dangerous commodity, and this fact must always be considered. Information can result in knowledge and power and, as such, its use must be closely monitored. The type of information that tends to be broadcast as an information slot does not usually lead one to think of this problem, but it must be considered. One example of the dilemmas that there can be in issuing information is that of the introduction of the gas and electricity meter rotas on Radio Sheffield. When this service was introduced there was much discussion at the station and with the local advisory board over the dangers that might be encountered by giving this information out over the public radio. However, it was decided that, on balance, the advantage, for the elderly in particular, of knowing where the genuine meter readers were going to be, and thus alerting them to unofficial callers, outweighed any disadvantages of the unofficial callers also knowing where the meter readers were expected, and using this to their advantage.

## Information presentation

The third action that is required in making an information slot is that of presenting the information, and this was the area of major emphasis for the research project. The research covered various aspects of the presentation of the slots, in particular, how well did the slot attract attention and stand out from the rest of the broadcast, was there a jingle associated with the information slot and was this a good idea? Was music playing in the background at the same time as the information was read out? How clear and how understandable was the information, and how did the presenter sound when reading it out. The usefulness, or otherwise, of an expert, or different presenter, reading out the information was also questioned. A further question was asked to find out if the public thought they knew when they would be able to obtain this sort of information from the radio, and if they thought that it was publicised enough.

The first major point to consider is the question of when to broadcast. Information slots are either announced regularly, or irregularly, on the radio, depending on their importance to the radio station and on their information content. The two major forms of information slot, the travel and weather news, tend to be broadcast on a regular basis on all radio stations. For example, on Radio Sheffield there is a travel bulletin every half hour and the weather is given out hourly along with the news bulletin. This allows the listeners to become used to when this information is going to be broadcast and helps to give a structure to the radio programme overall. However, because of the immediacy of the information, there are also times when this information should be, and often is, broadcast at another time, when the information will be of most use to the listeners (for example, a road or rail accident leading to long delays). This irregular method of broadcast does mean that the information may be missed by those who need it. This is a problem that the more ephemeral information slots have to contend with when they are, as is usual, broadcast irregularly. For example, the local events information was read out on Radio Sheffield whenever the presenter wished. The survey showed that the public found this a difficult information slot to catch on all local radio stations. Altogether 44 per cent stated that they definitely did not know when the information was broadcast, and the comments that accompanied included those such as 'depends on what you're doing. You could miss it'. The decision whether to broadcast slots on a regular or irregular basis will have to be made by the individual station and will depend on the overall programming policy. At the time that the survey was carried out, Radio Sheffield was attempting to make the programming more fluid with less specific junctions. The information contained within the slot will also affect the decision. For example, the pollen count can be naturally associated with the weather news and as this is a basic information slot, will be broadcast on a regular basis. The lost pets information can, if need be, be broadcast on a more irregular basis, because the information is only important to a very small number of people, although even here there is a case for a regular broadcast so that, if listeners have lost or found a pet, they will know when to switch on the radio.

The time of day also has a strong bearing on when the slot is broadcast. All stations tend to have more information slots in the early morning between seven and nine o'clock. On Radio Sheffield this is when the regular travel bulletins are broadcast, when the more extensive weather news (that from the actual weather centre) is announced, when the gas and electricity meter rotas are read out and also when the presenters make a special effort to announce the time fre-

quently. There are various reasons for this. One is that this is
a time when most people switch on their radios, often for this
very information, and also this is when the information is
most needed for the listeners to plan their day, for example to
use the weather news to decide what to wear. The survey
found that most people did, in fact, listen at this time of day:
85 per cent said that they heard most useful information in
the morning, with 74 per cent actually stating the 'early
morning'.

Apart from when the information is broadcast, there has to
be some attempt to make the information attract the listeners'
attention, or the whole reason for using slots will be lost.
There are various ways that this can be done and again these
will depend on whether the information slot is broadcast
regularly or irregularly. Many radio stations use independent
experts to present the information: the most common case is
that of the presenters from the weather centres. There are
various benefits and problems with this. One of the main
benefits is that having someone else to read out the information makes the information stand out well from the rest of
the broadcast. It also gives the information the stamp of
expert approval. In other words, it may appear to be more
accurate and important. For local stations, there is the added
advantage that it makes the station appear more local if the
expert is from the local area; for example, Radio Sheffield
used to use a British Rail employee from Sheffield station to
give information about the rail situation. For radio stations
that aim to represent and be part of a community, it is
important to use people from that community, and information slots can be a useful way of doing this. The survey
found that, of those people who thought that having an
independent expert was a good idea, the main reason given
was that they would have more knowledge about the information. The public would think both that the information was
more extensive and that the use of an expert gives a
legitimacy to the information.

The survey also pointed out that the major problem with
having local experts was that they tend not to be professional
broadcasters. The words 'amateurish' and 'distracting' were
used to describe them, and, as one respondent put it, 'they
might be an expert, but they are not a broadcaster'. Overall,
the public were not very keen on having independent experts

for any of the slots, but this was because of their lack of presentation skills. One solution may be to have the information slot read out by a different presenter from the normal one, so that the information is made distinct from the rest of the broadcast and therefore attracts attention, but is still clear and understandable. The survey found that this was quite a popular idea with 74 per cent of respondents thinking this where travel slots are concerned. But again, the overall programme has to be considered, for there may be times when having a different voice will break up the programme too much. There is also the problem that a lot of listeners become attached to the particular programme presenters, and would treat the information more seriously if it came from them rather than from someone else.

Many radio stations use jingles and musicial advertisements to make certain parts of their programmes stand out and attract attention, and many have them for specific information slots, usually the more fundamental ones such as the travel and weather news. The main problem with jingles is that they tend to be quite tiresome and their over-use can be a problem. The survey found that quite a high proportion of the listeners actively disliked jingles: the majority did concede that they would attract attention, but possibly only to make them switch off. Comments associated with this included 'get on your nerves' and 'would attract attention'. Jingles make a greater impact on a speech-based station, as their musical element makes them stand out. In this case, because the information slot is speech-based, they would not be very effective. However, the sort of people who listen to a speech-based radio station would be more likely to dislike this method.

A similar method to using a jingle is that of combining an advertisement with a particular information slot. Radio Hallam had incorporated an advertisement with the weather news in a further attempt to publicise this information (and pay for it). A business would sponsor the weather news for a period of time, and an advertisement for this firm would be broadcast before and after the weather news. One of the respondents mentioned that this made the information stand out well from the rest of the broadcast. However, it is also possible to argue that, on a station where there is a great deal of advertisement sponsoring, a specific information slot might not be an advantage, because it would not make the slot significantly different from the rest of the broadcast.

This problem of making the information stand out too much from the rest of the broadcast does mean that some stations attempt to bring some sort of overall cohesion to the programme. One way of doing this, particularly on a music-based station, is to play music in the background when the information is being announced. This, however, can be distracting, and for those hard of hearing will cause problems. The survey found that this was not a popular idea. Indeed, several of the elderly respondents commented that their hearing meant that this would make the information harder to hear. 'I'm pretty deaf and I can't catch both'. The general opinion was that playing music like this would be distracting; as one respondent put it 'you can't listen to two things at once'. Those who were not so against this idea tended to be younger and also those who listened to the radio for music anyway. One respondent said that the music would keep them interested whilst the information was on.

Once the station has succeeded in attracting the listeners' attention to the slot, it has to present the information in a clear and appropriate way. How the presenter sounds when reading out this information is therefore extremely important. One way that local stations attempt to make their broadcast seem local is to use a presenter with a local accent, and the survey found that this was generally appreciated by the public. 'Not Sheffielders, but I think they're Yorkshire. I like to hear the local accent'. However, a very broad local accent can have a negative effect, in that it can make the information harder to hear for the non-locals. This is particularly important if the information is aimed at these groups, such as the travel news bulletins for motorway traffic on Radio Sheffield.

The clarity of the information can also be a problem when the information to be read out consists of repetitive sounding lists. The presenters have a hard time making it sound interesting and, not surprisingly, often want to get this part of the broadcast over quickly. Some have the problem that they are reading out local names, such as street names on the gas and electricity rotas, of which they do not know the correct pronunciation. Indeed, one respondent commented that 'it can become a bit of a gabble, they race through places and it was only understandable if you were listening for a particular place', and another 'because it comes out like a list and so each bit of it doesn't stand out clearly from the others'. However, the list format is useful, because it is so different from the majority of radio output that this makes it stand out and attract attention. It was this principle that was used as the main means of attracting attention to the local events information on both Radio Sheffield and Radio Hallam, and 65 per cent of the respondents thought that it stood out well from the rest of the broadcast.

A very important aspect of the presentation of the information slots is how the presenter comes across to the listeners. The survey extracted a vast range of descriptions for the presenters. However what was conclusive was that the information they were reading affected how they read it. For example, if the weather forecast was for fine weather, they tended to be cheerful and so on. This was much appreciated by listeners. The survey also found that how the listeners were feeling at the time also affected how they heard the information slot, and how the presenter sounded to them. This was particularly true of the pollen count; from a hay fever sufferer came the comment 'One or two of them tend to gloat — perhaps they don't suffer. It is not something I'd wish on anybody'. Also the type of show within which the slot was presented tended to influence how the presenter came across. For example, one respondent talking about the Travel and Traffic news said 'All sound flippant. Doesn't matter, very friendly'.

There are some general problems that radio stations have in presenting information slots. The main one is that, by making each information slot stand out and attract attention, the broadcast could become overwhelmed by this form. It presents a particular problem on the local stations which tend to have a greater variety of these slots. The other problem is that, by broadcasting them more often and on a regular basis so that the listeners will not miss the information, there may be difficulties in breaking up the rest of the broadcast.

One of the major problems encountered in presenting information slots is that they tend to be regarded as programme fillers. Because the information is always available, particularly with slots such as the local events and lost pets, they are an ideal way for the presenter to cover a few spare seconds in

the programme. However, this can mean that such information tends to become regarded as a programme filler first
and foremost. The stations have to be very careful that, if the
information is used as a programme filler, then the actual
information slot is not ignored. The station must never come
to regard the programme filler as an effective means of
transferring the information, for, as the survey indicated, the
irregular broadcasts are only effective at reaching the people
already listening. Only when the information is announced
on a regular basis will the listener be able to switch on for that
sort of information.

Overall, the survey found that whatever way the information is presented is less important than the actual content
of the information. If the information was interesting and
useful, then it would attract the listeners' attention anyway.
For example, the travel and traffic information did not stand
out for those that were not interested in it. A comment about
the local events information was 'I think really it's when the
content is interesting that it attracts my attention. I don't
think there is something particular about the style or presentation that attracts'. This opinion was predominant across all
the information slots and radio stations. Yet this highlights a
problem that is fundamental to this kind of research on this
form of information: that the listeners would not know if they
had missed any information, and therefore they are only able
to give answers about the information slots that have been
successful in attracting and holding their attention. In order
to obtain more than just individual opinions, it would be
necessary to carry out a more objectively-based study.

## Concluding remarks

Local radio has proved to be a very important form of media
for the type of information that is broadcast as an information slot. A major element of this is its informal nature and
its accessibility. It is, for example, a great deal easier to switch
on the radio than to go in search of the information elsewhere.
The radio is also accessible to all regardless of their
intellectual skill and capabilities. Finding the information out
from the radio does not require great reading and compre-
hension skills, or knowledge of how to search the other public

information systems, such as the local library or newspaper. The radio is also more accessible in that it does not demand the recipients' full attention all the time, whereas print information requires the recipients to use their full concentration in absorbing the information. The radio is also designed to use only one of the senses, listening, whereas the television is designed to use both one's listening and sight senses. The survey showed that most people switched on the radio for background noise, rather than for specific information. People do tend to listen to the television, or listen to the radio, whilst performing other tasks; but the fact that the radio is designed to use only the one sense, and one that does not depend on location, means that it will be more effective at presenting the information to this type of user, rather than the television where various elements of the information will be lost. An example of this would be the weather news which, on the television, uses both sound and pictures to get its message across, whereas the radio weather forecast is designed to be understandable and clear without the use of pictures. The radio also has the advantage of being an up-to-date medium, and it has the opportunity to bring current information to the user, listener, quickly and efficiently. It is also able to update the information at frequent intervals, whereas other media, such as local papers, can only update the information daily.

The general public recognises that the radio is where to find the sort of information that is broadcast as an information slot. The majority (71 per cent) of the respondents to the public survey stated, at the beginning of the interview, that they heard useful information on the radio. Out of the other 29 per cent, only 1.6 per cent thought that this type and form of information was not important and should not be broadcast. The overwhelming opinion from the survey was that the immediate community information, the information slots, were important, with only one out of sixty-three stating that this form of information was not important. It was also found that the public thought that this form of information was particularly important on local radio, probably more so than on the national network radio, because of the immediacy and local nature of the information broadcast this way. 'It's very important on the local radio. It's the thing that ought to distance it from other network stations. Without it you may as well be listening to Radio Two', and 'it is important because I think local radio has got to service the community. People do need information and there are people who don't know how to go about getting information'. In fact, the audience ratings for local radio stations dramatically increase in times of extreme weather conditions and local crises. Therefore, at this time, the station has to cater for two audiences: the normal audience who knows what to expect from that radio station and the new audience who are unused to that station. This is always thought of by the stations as a good time to attract new listeners, and a lot of effort is, at this point, put into the information slots part of the broadcast. It is easier for the presenters in this sort of case, because it is clear to them that they are participating in the local community, and that the information slots are extremely important.

The importance that the public places on the provision of this type of information, as well as the advantages of using the radio, makes it imperative that this form of service is continued, and one needs to be aware of the political, social, and economic pressures that threaten public service broadcasts. There does, however, need to be some consideration of the problems inherent in having a national and a network radio system operating within the same area, often in co-operation, but sometimes in competition. The real question is when does the local stop and the national begin? Although information from the local stations is fed into the national network, this can at times seem over-dominated by the London and South-East news. With the recent financial pressures coming harder on the local stations, and with a proportionately higher drop in revenue than for the national stations, this may become an increasing problem.

To conclude — the research suggests that the information slots are vital to local radio and that local radio is the most accessible medium by which this type of information can be transferred. In order for these to be as useful, as informative and as enjoyable as possible, the fundamental reasons for the existence of local radio should be taken into account. As Winston Cooper, a presenter from Radio Sheffield, said:

> The main purpose of local radio is to reflect what affects the community, what is happening in the community and the views of the community. I think you should reflect both the problems and tastes of the people you serve, that you want to serve.

## Acknowledgements

We wish to thank the following for their help in the completion of this work: Mr G. Williamson, BBC Radio Sheffield and British Broadcasting Corporation Broadcasting Research Department, London.

## References

Connolly, F. (1990) 'Rebel pilots of the airwaves', *Guardian*, 20 August

European Society Opinion Market Research (1984) *Seminar on media research: does it really affect planning?* Lisbon (Portugal) 14–15 April, European Society Opinion Market Research

Fiddick, P. (1987) 'Local chiefs fight for the high ground' *Guardian*, 9 March

Francis R. (1985) 'Public service broadcasting: in whose interest are we broadcasting', *The Listener,* **23** (May), pp. 8–9

Green, H. C. (1960) *The BBC as a public service: three speeches*, BBC, London

Home Office (1987) *Radio: choices and opportunities: a consultative document,* Command Paper 92c, Home Office, London

Lewis, P. M. and Booth, J. (1990) *The invisible medium*, Macmillan

Martin, A. F. (1988) *Immediate community information on the local radio: a report of the public's perception of the information slots broadcast on the radio*, University of Sheffield, Sheffield

Nemiroff, J. and Linke, R. (1982) 'Consumer use of a household information hot-line generated by radio public service advertisements and other callers' preferences for consumer information sources', *Proceedings: 28th annual conference of the American Council on Consumer Interests*, American Council Consumer Interests

Radio Sheffield *BBC Radio Sheffield: A guide to your Local Radio Advisory Council,* BBC Radio Sheffield, Sheffield

Stone, S. (1984) *CRUS Guide: 6 Interviews*, British Library Board

Volunteer Centre Media Project (1980) *Media Project News,* Berkhamsted

Volunteer Centre Media Project (1982) *Advice-giving through local radio*, Social Action and the Media no. 12, Berkhamsted

Young, R. (1985) 'Aches and pains of weather forecasts', *The Times*, 31 January

# CHAPTER 5

# Education and personal information skills

## Jack Meadows

### Introduction

For most people their first, and often their only, formal introduction to information skills is at school. Certainly, it is here that most learn the skills of communicating in large groups. Similarly, providing an understanding of computers and, more generally, of information technology, is a task which is already devolving onto schools. The main theme in this chapter will be how satisfaction of this need is affecting thinking about the curriculum of the future. This breaks down into two parts. The first involves an analysis of what steps have already been taken within the curriculum, and what trends may be expected to appear in the immediate future. The second examines how well these trends will satisfy future ability to handle personal information in an increasingly computerised world.

A cartoon published some years ago showed a man wide-eyed with excitement. The caption underneath said, 'I have seen the future and it goes beep, beep, beep'. Since at least the 1960s, educationalists have seen a somewhat similar computerised vision of the future. Progress was slow initially. The 1960s was an era of mainframe computers which were not well adapted to schoolteaching. Worthwhile experiments such as the PLATO (Programmed Logic for Automatic Training

Operations) system in the USA, which linked classroom terminals to a central mainframe, were set up, and indicated something of the value of computers for teaching. More commonly, schools situated near higher education establishments were allowed to use the latters' computers for a few minutes a week, mainly for pupils specialising in science.

The cost and lack of flexibility of mainframes told against them. In addition, the early experiments with computers took place during the same period that educational technology was receiving great attention in the educational world. Disappointment with educational technology, because it did not — indeed could not — live up to the hype that originally accompanied it, led for a while to a reaction against computer-aided teaching, and not only against the audio-visual techniques then forming the core of educational technology. Consequently, the first signs of the potential interest of computers for all types and ages of pupils came from outside schools. The sudden mania for computer games at the end of the 1970s took many adults by surprise. Some of their dire warnings about the consequences resembled condemnations of children's comics in earlier decades. As with comics, the actual impact varied from child to child but, for some at least, it led to a wider interest in computers.

## The microcomputer

The catalyst for the rapid change of attitude was the advent of the microprocessor. This both brought the cost of computing within the range of most schools, and provided a much more flexible teaching aid. In the UK, the breakthrough occurred with the commissioning of the BBC micro and its rapid distribution to schools. Micros changed the direction of thinking. They were called 'personal' computers, because it was recognised that, unlike mainframe computers (or the later developed minicomputers), they essentially catered for the individual, rather than the group. The focus of the mainframe was institutional, whereas the micro could be used by the individual at home.

The appearance and rapid development of the micro naturally led to an extensive discussion of its socio-economic significance. It soon became accepted that some level of 'computer literacy' would be essential for most citizens in the future. This conclusion necessarily brought governments into the discussion. How they reacted varied from country to country. In the USA, the early commercial leader in the micro field, Apple, promoted the idea that manufacturers who donated computers to schools should benefit from tax concessions. In the UK, the government launched a 'micros in schools' campaign, which negotiated a half-price agreement for school purchases of Acorn computers. Most schools took up this offer. More imaginatively, over two hundred information technology centres were established to provide young people with hands-on experience of the new technology. The French government entered the field a little after the USA and UK — in the mid-1980s — but then, in a sweeping gesture, decided to put well over 100,000 micros into the French school system.

This recognition that micros were going to make an impact on life outside school, as well as on schoolteaching, in the near future was obviously correct. But these major initiatives had drawbacks, as well as advantages. In the UK, for example, relating the school programme to a particular manufacturer meant not only that the hardware could be obtained cheaply, but also that an adequate amount of software would be prepared to support it. This advantage has been somewhat offset by the failure of other areas of education, and of the outside world, to use the same hardware and software. Consequently, a gap opened up between what was learned at school and what was experienced elsewhere.

## Micros and information technology

The rapid diffusion of micros through schools soon led to a realisation of administrative problems in their use for teaching. Two examples — still important — can be mentioned by way of illustration. The first relates to the distribution and use of the equipment in different types of school. Even if the initial distribution is even-handed, it rarely remains that way. Many schools supplement their resources by persuading their parents' organisations to buy additional equipment. This is obviously more likely to occur in areas where parents are relatively wealthy and interested in education. It is also easier to attract teachers with computing interests into these schools. The result is that imbalances between schools in the use of computers tend to establish themselves and to be perpetuated. The second example relates to the use of computers. Their initial applications in secondary schools were for science teaching, especially in mathematics and the physical sciences. These tend to be male-dominated subjects in mixed schools, and the image of computing as a masculine pursuit still persists to some extent today.

The changing ideas of what micros can be used for are reflected, in part, by the appearance of the phrase 'information technology'. Initially, the emphasis in computer development was on the technology — the hardware and the software. Now the emphasis is shifting to the information. It is here that interaction with teaching becomes most fruitful. This broadening is apparent in the various definitions of information technology (IT) that circulate in the educational world. For example:

> IT is the acquisition, production, transformation, storage and transfer of data (information) by electronic means — in forms such as vocal, pictorial, textual and numeric — so as to facilitate interactions between people and between people and machines. IT also includes the applications and implications (social, economic and cultural) of these processes.[1]

As this definition indicates, the focus of information technology covers much more than the micro alone. There are input devices, such as the mouse, and output devices, such as the printer. Storage devices, such as CD-ROM, and teaching facilities, such as interactive video, are becoming increasingly important ancillaries; and so on. Despite the rapid growth in what teachers can expect of information technology, it is still likely that IT will supplement human teaching in schools, rather than replace it. This is reflected in many of the names applied to the process of using information technology in teaching. 'Computer-assisted learning' (CAL) is probably the commonest, but 'aided', 'based', or 'enhanced' may replace 'assisted'. Similarly, 'instruction', 'education', 'training', or 'teaching' may occur instead of 'learning'.

## Computer-assisted learning

There have been many discussions of how CAL fits into the overall process of education. It has been suggested, for example, that four different paradigms exist.[2] The first is the 'instructional paradigm'. This sees computers as basically providing programmed learning. The computer contains the material to be learnt, each item of which is retrieved and studied sequentially. Progress from one item to the next depends on satisfactory learning at each stage. Next comes the 'emancipatory paradigm'. This supposes that the micro is there to reduce the drudgery, so that pupils can concentrate on the more important parts of the learning process. (An example is the use of a micro to carry out a long sequence of computations.) The 'revelatory paradigm' supposes that the important aspect is for the pupil to learn by discovery. New information and underlying theory are progressively revealed as the pupil interacts with the micro. For example, the computer may provide a simulation of an experiment through which pupils must find their way. The final approach envisages a 'conjectural paradigm', implying that pupils, in a sense, create their own knowledge. The job of the micro is then mainly to help pupils test their ideas.

It is, of course, possible to teach computing as a subject in its own right. That apart, the various possibilities really fall into two groups. The first is concerned with the use of computers as tools to supplement the learning process traditionally pursued in schools. The second sees computers as a new category of teaching aid which offers the opportunity for major innovation in the learning process. Activities of the first type are now firmly established: they are relatively easy to devise and integrate readily into the school curriculum. The second group still raises some basic queries regarding their construction and their use in the classroom. Looking outward from the school, most automated devices currently encountered in everyday life fall in the first category (although many commentators suppose that devices based on the second type of approach will become increasingly popular in the future).

'Computer-managed learning' reflects a rather different area where micros have established their value. In this, the computer is applied to managing the teaching process, rather than providing teaching directly. The term actually covers two different topics. The first involves planning — selecting appropriate courses, devising schedules, and so on. The second is concerned with the assessment of progress. Computers have, of course, been used for years to help with educational administration. The interest of these new developments is that they are aimed at personal, rather than institutional, management. This new flexibility, which directs attention at the individual rather than the group, has important implications for all aspects of teaching.

## Micros and the teaching process

Curriculum development using information technology has been identified as an area of major educational significance in all developed countries. For example, the Development of European Learning by Technological Advance (DELTA) project has been established within the EC for this purpose. The initial question is obvious — what are the particular virtues of computers as a medium for education? Many attempts have been made to list the requirements for successful implementation of CAL. The topics[3] can be summarised in the following list:

1. The pupil must be motivated to learn with a micro. This covers not just willingness to use a micro (although microphobia still exists), but also having a clear idea of the purpose of using a micro. It is evident that pupils learn best when they can see an immediate and obvious objective. One of the good things about computer games is that no-one doubts the objective — to zap the space invader before it zaps you. In teaching, objectives may be hard to explain because the pupils do not initially have the knowledge needed to understand them. Micros can help here by establishing intermediate objectives (including learning about micros themselves).
2. Pupils are helped if they are given a quick reminder of what they know already before they progress on to new material. Up to the present, most micro-based teaching programs have not provided such background. However, computer programs do have the obvious virtue that pupils can return to them as often as they wish. Hence, as CAL comes in at all levels of schools, pupils should be able to return to lower-level material that they have already met.
3. Teaching should stimulate pupils *en route* to their final objec-

tives. Micros do this fairly well at present, since they are still seen as a little novel and exciting. Even if this feeling wears off with experience, the trend towards multi-media interactive learning should provide additional stimulation in the future.

4. Meaningful learning requires active participation by the pupil, rather than passive reception of knowledge. Here, a well-designed computer package can often win all down the line, as compared with (say) reading a textbook, in terms of interaction.

5. Most pupils need good feedback on their progress when they venture into new fields. Micros can score heavily here, too. They not only provide immediate feedback, but can often do so without embarrassing a learner who is wrong. Micros are obviously a very long way from providing the quality of response achieved by a human teacher. Nevertheless, their level of interaction with users is becoming rapidly more sophisticated.

6. Many areas of learning entail repetition and practice. Computers obviously come off well in this respect, since, unlike human teachers, they never become bored. But some degree of sophistication is essential, as the sort of errors made by pupils may change from the initial to later stages of learning.

7. How well-established media, such as textbooks, are used normally depends on the teacher, who decides which sections shall be tackled and in what sequence. Microcomputer programs are liable to impose their own logic regarding the sequencing of material to be taught. From the learning viewpoint, this can be a good or a bad trait, depending on how well the computer package has been prepared.

8. Finally, there is the question of opportunities provided for creativity. It might be said that reading textbooks and writing essays are linked, since information from the former feeds into the latter. In other words, identification and retrieval of information from books is linked with the creative activity of writing. The link between absorbing and creating is often still closer with computers. Partly this is because the two activities are, in this case, both carried out on the same item of equipment. More importantly, the exploration of new concepts or activities via computers can be more readily designed to be carried out in an intellectually creative way.

A glance through the foregoing list of factors that affect computer use reveals an interesting point. Under each heading, a micro could, in principle, operate independently of a human teacher. Although a long-term teaching aim may be to achieve that goal, caution is needed at present. Computer packages can still be inflexible and unsophisticated. In addition, expectations of how pupils will use a particular teaching program may prove to be wrong. Above all, pupils need continuous and extended hands-on contact with micros in order to use them effectively. This is still not possible in schools, and the number of pupils with home computers, although growing, is still relatively small. A comparison can be drawn here with books in the home. Children who come from homes where reading is regarded as important have advantages in terms of literacy; correspondingly, homes where computing is accepted should help with computer literacy.

## The approach to CAL

Along with increasing knowledge of the actual mechanics of applying computers to teaching, there is a growing, if still controversial, body of theory relating to CAL. An example of this interaction between practice and theory is provided by the computer language LOGO (from the Greek 'logos' — 'reason'), developed in the United States by Seymour Papert and others. Papert had worked previously with the Swiss psychologist, Jean Piaget, whose ideas have had a major impact on educational thought during the past few decades. LOGO uses very simple commands to allow children to explore mathematical ideas visually, on a computer screen, or with a robot 'turtle' on the floor. Papert has explained his approach in the following terms.[4]

> In many schools today, the phrase 'computer-aided instruction' means making the computer teach the child. One might say the *computer is being used to program the child.* In my vision, *the child programs the computer* and, in doing so, both acquires a sense of mastery over a piece of the most modern and powerful technology and establishes an intimate contact with some of the deepest ideas from science, from mathematics, and from the art of intellectual model-building.

> Two fundamental ideas run through this book. The first is that it is possible to design computers so that learning to communicate with them can be a natural process, more like learning French by living in France than like trying to learn it through the unnatural process of American foreign-language instruction in classrooms. Second, learning to communicate with a computer may change the way other learning takes place. The computer can be a mathematics-speaking and an alphabetic-speaking unity. We are learning how

to make computers with which children love to communicate. When this communication occurs, children learn mathematics as a living language.

The approach discussed here by Papert ultimately relates to the nature of the interface between the computer and the pupil: in the sense that it should permit pupils to impose themselves on computers rather than the reverse. There has been much recent discussion of the role of expert systems in providing for such an interface. Such systems should permit users to approach computers at their own level of knowledge (or ignorance) and yet still extract the information they need. For example, expert systems are now available to guide users through legislation, so that they can extract its significance for their own personal needs. Legal problems are moderately straightforward in computer terms, since they are typically intended to be solved by a rules-based approach (But see also Chapter 2). One difficulty with more open-ended questions, such as are found in many school subjects, is that experts on these matters themselves often find it hard to agree on what the appropriate answers should be. Indeed, current explorations of expert systems in education suggest that widespread use will be hindered by a lack of understanding of the learning process together with uncertainties in the diagnosis of errors on the part both of teachers and learners. For the immediate future, the value of work on expert systems may actually lie in defining more clearly what is, and what is not, sound teaching technique.

Analysis of computer-based activities in the classroom indicates that teachers typically use computers for a limited number of purposes. The most frequent appear to be (1) using micros as a tool co-ordinated with other classroom activities, e.g. to develop information-handling skills across a variety of subjects; (2) to emphasise computer awareness and appreciation; (3) to provide special applications for particular subjects; in that order. One study in the UK found that staff thought the main virtues of micros were to improve motivation, increase familiarity with computing and reinforce ordinary teaching methods.[5] The main disadvantages noted were insufficient access to micros and poor-quality software. As this suggests, most current comments see the value of information technology in terms of its impact on the educational process, whereas the defects relate primarily to lack of resources. In this latter respect, pupils who have access to micros out of school hours can obviously benefit. Furthermore, the type of micro-based teaching provided seems to vary systematically with ability level: the lower the pupils' ability, the greater the emphasis on basic skills only. The less able pupils would therefore benefit from more exposure to micros than other children, but they are often the group least likely to get it.


## Information technology and the curriculum

On the larger scale, discussions of teaching method merge into questions about the curriculum. The role of information technology naturally depends on how curriculum development is envisaged. At the simplest level, two views of the curriculum can be distinguished. The 'classical' tradition emphasises a rational, structured approach, whilst the 'romantic' tradition is more concerned with a diversified, relatively unstructured approach. At first sight, information technology would seem to fit better into the first tradition. The initial use of micros in schools — to cater for science and mathematics — illustrates this approach. However, present trends in computer use increasingly fit in with an individualistic approach. For example, even simple word-processing allows for individual decisions on the handling of text; the more recent development of desk-top publishing allows for far more self-expression. The growing ability to handle computer graphics and multi-media on micros will expand this flexibility. Hence, information technology cannot be said to be intrinsically biased toward either type of approach to the curricula. It is true that the rational tradition has often been easier to implement, but networking (discussed below) may alter this.

Over the past few years, considerable attention has been devoted to the idea of a 'core curriculum' in the UK and elsewhere. Such core curricula are typically supposed to cover virtually every principle. In the UK, for example, they are sometimes said to be concerned with the aesthetic, the creative, the ethical, the linguistic, the mathematical, the physical, the political, the scientific, the social and the spiritual. In practice, implementation of a core curriculum may emphasise some approaches to teaching more than others. Responsibility for deciding on methodology may be partly taken out of the teacher's hands. Assessment is usually by achievement of a certain standard over a defined range of subjects. Hence, the introduction of a core curriculum can tend to emphasise the rational, structured aspect of computer usage.

To be set against this is the rapidly increasing flexibility of information technology. The devisers of the new British 'national curriculum' have decided that some aspects of IT should be explicitly taught, whilst others should be integrated into other subject teaching. Working groups set up to examine the different subject areas have been asked to look at the role of IT in their portion of the curriculum. This means that they have to consider three questions. To what extent is IT a basic element determining the nature of the curriculum? What specific IT-related skills might it be appropriate to introduce into their particular subject area? What role can IT play in helping pupils in that subject area to retrieve and record information? From the viewpoint of future educational use of IT, the first question is obviously fundamental. Unfortunately, owing particularly to the present lack of IT resources, most attention is currently concentrated on the latter two questions. Indeed, there is some room for fearing that IT will simply be seen in many classrooms as a facilitating device (like hand-held calculators in mathematics), rather than as something that may fundamentally change life within the school and outside.

The stated government policy in the UK is to have at least one micro for every 60 primary pupils and at least one for every 30 secondary pupils. This is a more generous average than currently exists in many Western countries, but it has to be set against the curriculum target that every pupil will need to know and understand ways in which information can be gathered, interpreted and used in decision-making and how information can be stored in, organised by, retrieved from and displayed by a computerised system. In these terms, the resources are likely to remain overstretched.

The one subject in the British national curriculum which is identified as having information technology as a central concern is 'design and technology'. This course is intended to ensure that pupils develop a broad understanding of IT,

including its applications and its social and economic importance. Attainment targets and their assessment in this subject
are therefore of particular significance in forecasting what
knowledge of IT the general population of the UK will have in
years to come. It is currently expected that the average 16-
year old will be able to use IT to identify and capture the
information needed for specified tasks, to create a database
from this information, to extract information efficiently in
response to enquiries and to present such information
selectively and in an appropriate form. Suggested suitable
projects include creating a database about land use and
landowners in the neighbourhood of the school, or setting up
an enquiry system to answer questions about the school
timetable.

Information technology has been defined as the combination of computers with telecommunications. So far, in this
chapter, the discussion has concentrated on computers; but
the ability to interact is an essential facet of IT for education.
The linking of computers via networks is therefore expected to
be a growth area in educational computing. A range of
networks are already available to schools. For example, one
well-established British network for schools is Campus 2000.
This provides the usual range of networked services — electronic mail, a bulletin board and access to databases — although
the system has been as much used by teachers and school
authorities for administrative purposes, as it has by pupils for
educational ones. However, like most networks, it is linked to
other networks, and this has already given some idea of the
potential of networking for education. The European Studies
Project, run from the UK, is an example. One of its activities
links schools in the UK with others in Belgium, Eire, France
and elsewhere. The pupils exchange information via the
network on an agreed list of topics in geography and history.
The basic idea is that they should be able to see the same
questions from the viewpoint of other countries; but there is
an obvious further spin-off in terms of the IT and linguistic
skills learnt. Various similar projects link schools in other
countries. For example, the Intercultural Learning Network
connects Illinois, California, Tokyo and Jerusalem.

In educational terms, the different services provided by a
network cater for different needs. Electronic mail supposes a
one-to-one contact (although the 'one' may be a group of

people). A bulletin board provides a central store of information which anyone can read or add to. However, much recent discussion of electronic communication between schools has concentrated on computer conferencing. In this, each individual or group is in frequent and repeated contact with a limited number of other individuals or groups. As the word 'conferencing' implies, they are usually involved in discussing a common basic theme. There is a 'moderator', who supervises and organises the electronic discussion. This provides, in principle, a good model for one approach to network-based teaching. In practice, it requires a major input both of resources and of teaching effort, which may be difficult for schools to maintain.

## Post-school IT

Information technology is now seen as an important area of activity at both the primary and the secondary level. Primary schools have the particular significance that it is there children first make contact with computers (unless a computer is available at home). Hence, basic IT skills must be instilled at the primary school level. More advanced skills come later at the secondary level. Obviously, however, not all IT skills can be learned at school. In fact, IT teaching is more intensive and better resourced in higher and further education. This evidently implies that people who have experienced post-school education are likely to be better equipped to face the brave new world of information technology. Hence, the question occurs — how much IT training will be required to hold down a job in the future?

The impact of computer-based automation on jobs, especially in the manufacturing sector, is already evident. Automation has led to higher productivity and so to fewer jobs. The impact on white-collar occupations has been somewhat less evident. The reason is that the new technology has introduced new jobs, whilst removing others — something that has happened much less in traditional areas of manufacturing. The simple deduction from experience to date is that two types of job will provide the best bet for the future — those which involve activities that cannot readily be automated and those where human input to the technology is essential.

The service sector (catering, refuse collection, etc.) exemplifies the first group, whilst the latter includes almost all the professions. It remains unclear how schools can best provide an IT framework for these divergent career opportunities.

## IT in everyday life

This point leads to an even more crucial question. What basic education will be necessary so that all citizens can have access to information and activities in an increasingly IT-dominated future? It is evident, looking around, that the general public is already acclimatising itself to a range of IT-based devices. The automated teller machines (ATMs) at banks are an example of technology that most people (except some of the elderly) have accepted. Current developments will extend the range of facilities available via ATMs, but they already reflect some of the requirements for automation to be successful. The menu system used is simple and easily under-stood. Customers know how long a transaction will take using a machine and they have 24-hour-a-day access to services. From the bank's viewpoint, ATMs are equally valuable, since they save employees' time and so the bank's money. In principle, they should free time for employees to be involved in additional service activities: in practice, they may be used for savings on manpower.

ATMs are characteristic of many expected future develop-ments in IT because they are interactive. The same is true, although only in a limited sense, of another widely available service — teletext. In the UK, the two of this type available are Ceefax and Oracle. Access to them is typically via a television set, using a hand-held device which can retrieve page numbers as required. (Each 'page' corresponds to one screen-ful of information.) These services have proved quite popular, since they provide rapid updates of frequently wanted infor-mation — such as news, sport, weather and travel. Of course, one of the most commonly used forms of interactive IT is computer games. As these have taken aboard new develop-ments in IT, they have increasingly shown their potential for educational, as well as recreational use.

Alongside these directly interactive forms of IT, there are others where the interaction is observed, but not participated in. An obvious example is electronic point-of-sale (EPOS) equipment in shops, which typically uses laser scanners to read bar codes attached to the items purchased. Such equipment has advantages for customers (e.g. in speed of service), but they do not participate directly in its use. The same is true of borrowing books from a public library. It is convenient for customers to have a single card that they can use for any kind of borrowing, but it is the library assistant who actually uses the technology.

Finally, although far from least in importance, there is an increasing amount of information technology which impinges on everyday life, but is not immediately visible. Indeed, many people may not realise that it exists. This ranges from the electronic information systems currently being experimented with in hospitals to all kinds of official records, from driving licences to social welfare benefits (As described in previous chapters).

## School curricula and everyday life

Will the role of information technology in the school curriculum be such that the average school-leaver can cope subsequently with the demands of rapidly expanding IT-based activities? The prognosis here is fairly optimistic. If public facilities, such as ATMs, are to be successful, they must be user-friendly: otherwise, they will not be used. This means they must assume a low minimum of knowledge on the part of customers, and they must guide customers very carefully through whatever steps are required. Under these circumstances, the amount of IT experience now being incorporated into the school curriculum should be adequate to allow most school-leavers to keep up with new IT-based devices and facilities as they appear. However, those in the lowest socio-economic grouping, along with some who are mentally or physically handicapped, may well lose out. If activities currently carried out by intermediaries devolve onto end-users in the future, this judgement may need looking at again. For example, there has been an extended debate concerning the viability of 'home shopping'. In this, the customer sits at home, and can obtain information on, order and pay for a range of goods, using IT links. If a variety of goods and shops are involved, the level of interaction required can become quite complex. Should home shopping prove to be a viable option, along with other facilities of a similar level of complexity, it may reflect back on the teaching of IT skills required in schools.

It is, however, at the knowledge, rather than the skills, level that most queries accumulate. It is one thing, for example, to decree that people should have legal right of access to personal information about them which is held on computer files. It is quite another for an ordinary person to learn how to search out the relevant files and gain access to them. Not only can the steps involved be complex; they are, moreover, likely to change with time. The question of how to provide the average school pupil with an adequate background to tackle this type of problem is still being debated.

## Training for older people

Another question of immediate importance is whether those who finished full-time education before information technology became important now need to be helped in coping with it. The answer is linked, in part, with their educational background. Better educated people can cope more easily — as witness the link between the purchase of home computers and the educational level of the purchasers. In general, much IT that is likely to impinge on everyday life can probably be absorbed. However, elderly people, especially those in lower-income groups and with a lower level of education, may well find the rate at which new information technology devices are appearing very bewildering.

There are more serious difficulties in the workplace. At the one end come those whose jobs have disappeared owing to automation. At the other, equally important, are those whose jobs continue, but the jobs now require a level of IT knowledge that the occupants do not possess. All these are likely to require some degree if retraining. No doubt, traditional channels — short courses, longer courses in further education colleges, etc. — will continue to be there to help them. But information technology may itself help in the training. The growth in range and sophistication of interactive teaching devices will certainly continue. For example, considerable effort is currently going into such devices for user education as CD-I (compact disc-interactive). It can be expected that post-school institutions will be better able to exploit such devices more rapidly than schools, since their access to resources and staff/student ratios are generally better. One query for the future concerns the commercial use of information technology for training purposes. There has been an explosion in recent years in the commercial provision of short courses relating to information technology. Will post-school training through commercial channels become an increasingly significant part of the total provision for IT education?

One aspect of post-school education that has been extensively discussed is distance learning. Education of this sort can be applied when the student is geographically isolated from the teacher (and, usually, from other students). The growth of networking has led to an increasing interest in information technology as a means of alleviating the isolation of such students. Even in the UK, where distances are relatively small, distance education via networks should be able to be used to some advantage, especially where teaching is provided for a large area by a single institution. In large countries with a relatively low population density, such as Canada or Australia, IT-based distance learning could well become very important. Over such large distances, information technology now expands to cover communication via satellite. An example in Western Europe is the Olympus satellite, which will be used to test a range of multilingual distance education programmes. The problem with distance education is the amount of effort that must be expended in establishing and maintaining the courses. Where financial return is likely to be good — as in many IT-oriented topics — courses will be developed. Elsewhere, resources may prove too limited for rapid development of IT-based distance education.

## Conclusion

In summary, the role of information technology in schools of the future has been extensively discussed by educationalists. Some practical computer-based teaching in schools is now routine. However, limitations on resources of all kinds are

# CHAPTER 6

# Technology in and outside the home: its effects on the provision of personal information for living

## Howard Petrie

### Introduction

This chapter gives an overview of the use of technology in the home as it affects personal information provision. It discusses the use of audio equipment, the telephone, television and the personal computer, and the way each of them has affected information provision in the home. A discussion of audio equipment would not be complete without hi-fi equipment, tape recorders and the newer systems such as compact disc. The telephone is, first and foremost, a voice communication device, but it can be used to connect personal computers and terminals to computers as well. Other equipment, such as the facsimile transmission machines, can also be connected to telephone networks.

A discussion on television and information provision must include videotex (Prestel, Minitel, etc.) and teletext (Ceefax, Oracle). In addition, personal computers have progressed rapidly and now include a much wider range of functions than previously. For instance, at one time, few home computers had disc drives, as they made the machines too expensive for the mass market. Now machines with diskette drives are commonplace in the home and many have fixed (winchester) disc drives as well. The compact disc can be used in conjunction with a home computer, although in this form it has yet to penetrate the home market in any significant way.

This chapter concentrates on technology as it directly affects the equipment in the home itself. The provision of information in the home is very much affected by the application of technology outside it. For instance, the production of books, newspapers and magazines is very highly mechanised. To the consumer, they may look identical to products formerly produced by older methods, but without the technology many of them might now be too expensive to produce at all. The changes in some products are noticed by the consumer, for instance the increasing use of colour in newspapers. Before going to the main topic of the chapter, a brief summary of some of the major impacts of technology employed outside the home on personal information provision will be given.

The banks have been radically affected by information technology. Computers and communication systems provide instant information on the state of accounts and provide fast transfer of transactions between branches of the same bank and between different banks. One facet of this development is the plastic card: many people carry several of them in their wallets and handbags. Cards are used to withdraw money and to find out the status of an account from a cash dispenser on a 24-hours-a-day basis. Numerous credit cards are available, some of which can be used almost everywhere, whereas others can only be used in specific shops. Credit cards have radically changed the possibilities for shopping, providing quite amazing new possibilities for buying. For instance, the author recently bought some computer software from a mail order firm in New York. The advertisement came from an American computer magazine on sale in the UK. The order was placed by telephone, payment was by credit card and the item arrived in the post only two weeks later. There was a saving of more than 30 per cent on the price in the UK. Debit cards are also appearing which can be used in shops for purchases. The approach here is to debit the customer's account directly by connecting the point-of-sale terminal to the relevant bank computer.

With the introduction of information systems to the stock

exchange, the effect has been a more efficient brokerage service for the private investor. The banks and building societies have also increased their involvement in share dealings, providing share services to a wider public than hitherto.

The workplace is seeing a dramatic change in the use of information systems. It is widely believed that it will be essential for office workers to have a personal computer, or a terminal, on their desks. One effect of this is the growing expertise of the individual in the use of information systems. This is bound to have an effect in the home. The availability of personal computers in the home makes it easier to work there. The widespread use of the portable computer in the workplace has also helped to make this possible. It is not uncommon for employers to equip their staffs with portable machines, particularly those who are on the move, such as sales and marketing staff. These machines are then available, as is the software, for home use.

The important role played by information in business and industry is increasingly being recognised. It can be regarded as a resource, just as energy, human beings, transport, etc., are. The increased weight placed on the importance of information at work will draw the attention of the individual to its role in the home.

In the field of education, technology has recently been given high priority. Most schools have microcomputers and the teaching of information technology is being brought into more courses at university. Microcomputers are often available to students at a discount through university purchase programmes.

It is possible for some categories of workers to stay at home, at least for part of the working week. The personal computer and the telephone allow them to communicate with colleagues in the office or connect to relevant computers. Some small businesses are also operated from home, and small computers are usually to be found in these organisations. All these factors help to increase the availability of information systems in the home. They can then be used for personal information provision.

Improved communication and information systems have benefited the various media industries. Thus television, radio, the newspaper, publishing and printing industries, bookshops and libraries have been able to improve their products and/or services. Satellites and world-wide telecommunication networks have made it possible to see what is going on in other parts of the world as it happens. Details of worldwide stockmarkets prices and indices appear in detail in the financial press and are available directly from computers. Newspapers, such as *The Financial Times* are typeset and then transmitted to various places around the world. They are then printed locally and are available at the same time in different countries, at local competitive prices. Books can also be typeset in one country and printed in another at the other end of the world. Library catalogues and bibliographical databases are available online and on compact disc. Access to these databases is available in the home in some places. However, for the vast majority of users, it will be some time before these catalogues and databases are consulted from home.

Most organisations have embraced information technology, and it is widely spread in the workplace in many of them. An important question is whether this technology has reached the home, other than through the inevitable external technological pressures at work and in society outside the home? Spending on electronic equipment in the home in the USA has risen from 1.1 per cent of the family budget in 1980 to 1.6 per cent in 1989.[1] This represented (in 1989) $54.6 billion. Video-cassette recorders, CD players, cordless telephones, micro-computers, multiple television sets and portable audio-cassette players have come to be a requirement in many homes. What effect is this having on the provision of personal information? Each of these types of equipment is discussed below.

## Sound recording and reproduction

Sound reproduction equipment is available in almost every home. It takes different forms, some equipment being portable, other being static. The most common is the radio, programmes for which can be made and/or broadcast at a local, regional or national level, or come from other countries. Radio programmes can be made to be informative as well as, or instead of, being entertaining. The information content depends, of course, on the individual programme and on the listener. The Open University has radio broadcasts as well as those on television, both designed to support its courses. In the UK, the BBC and ITV also put out broadcasts for schools. Some radio stations have realised that the informing role is one that some television stations have neglected, and they are finding a market for in-depth news and current affairs broadcasts.

The media of magnetic tape, vinyl discs and compact discs (CD) are the main ones used in the home for the reproduction of recorded sound. Most of the discs purchased for the home are music, but some spoken discs are available. A common example is their use in the learning of foreign languages.

The developments in microelectronics have benefited the audio equipment used in the home. Sound reproduction has improved and the equipment has become more compact. The compact disc (CD) has a superior sound reproduction compared with previous recording media and it is smaller than the vinyl disc. An even more recent development than the CD is digital audio-tape (DAT), which provides the good quality of reproduction of the compact disc with the ability to record. DAT is also used as a personal computer peripheral, as is the compact disc. DAT, unlike the CD, has yet to become established in the market-place, and currently seems to be having difficulty doing so because of fears of illegal copying.[2]

## Television

A television set is found in almost every home. It is a central source of information, as well as providing entertainment. In addition to the 'normal' output, special programmes are put on in the UK by the Open University and by the BBC and ITV for schools. These programmes are, of course, available to the private viewer.

Satellite broadcasting has recently become established in the United Kingdom, as it has in many other Western countries. The number of available channels has therefore increased rapidly. Programmes put out for other countries are also available in the UK. Some channels are deliberately aimed at an international audience. Although there is a language barrier (the average viewer in the UK does not have a good command of other languages), the international programmes provide a different view of events, and other cultures are reflected in the output.

Satellite television looks as if it will be more successful in Europe than cable television, at least in the short term. The problem with the latter approach has been the large cost required to lay the cables in the first place. This is not the case in the United States where cable television is much more widely spread. Those areas that have been cabled have the flexibility to provide a large number of television channels. Only a few areas have been cabled in the United Kingdom. Where such cabling exists, larger numbers of local channels can be devoted to education, hobbies, specialist topics and news. This is particularly true in the United States.

The video-cassette recorder-player (VCR) is also widely used in the home. Video-cassettes with preset recordings can either be bought or rented, or home recordings can be made from television broadcasts. The recording function was the main reason why video tape has succeeded and the video disc (see below) has so far failed in the home market. The VCR provides an added source of information in the home. A popular example is the use of video recordings to help with home fitness training.

Television is usually operated as a basically one-way medium: consequently it is difficult to interact with it. An example of feedback is when voting for a favourite song performed in a televised competition by telephoning to an automatic vote counter. Two-way communication with television is available though cable: the television set can be equipped with a keyboard to allow the viewer to send data in the reverse direction. The transmission of data from the user to the information source can also be achieved by connecting a television keyboard directly to the telephone.

The Ceefax and Oracle systems in the UK are examples of broadcast information services, or Teletext. The available screens, or frames of information, are continually broadcast one after the other in the free space not required by normal programmes, and those frames required can be selected with the aid of a simple keypad. Teletext televisions are not much more expensive than those not so equipped, and the information itself is provided free of charge. These information systems have been very successful, largely due to the low cost to the consumer and the simplicity of use.

The future of television standards is under considerable discussion at present. The aim is to increase the quality of the television by improving picture quality, sound and by providing other features. These developments are commonly called high definition television (HDTV).[3] An example of the new facilities is the ability to view more than one programme simultaneously through different 'windows' — areas on the screen devoted to different topics. The idea is not unlike the windowing facility provided on personal computers. There is likely to be, in the longer term, increasing competition between the computer industry and the consumer electronics industry in the home television market. The former is becoming interested in computing involving sound and video, as well as the traditional text and graphics. An article by Gilder[4] argues that the future of television lies in 'telecomputing'. He believes that, with the ability to put in place broad bandwidth fibre optic cables, television services, based on multimedia computing, would be a better alternative than broadcast television. Users would be connected by cable to large tele-computers to obtain multimedia productions, and would be able to interact with programmes to obtain customised viewing. This could be, for instance, the ability to zoom in on a football game by selecting an alternative camera. Material for viewing could be selected from various databases and planned in advance. For instance, the viewer might decide to see the French news at 6 o'clock, do an interactive cookery course at 6.30 and watch a newly released film at 7.30. The viewer would, with world-wide networks in place, have access to material from anywhere in the world.

## The telephone

Only a few years ago, the telephone service in the UK, as in many other countries, was operated by the national Post Office (known in many countries as the PTT). The British Post Office (BPO) saw its main telecommunications role as the provision of telephone and telegraph services. Today, things are very different: not only has the telecommunications side of the BPO been sold off as a private company

(British Telecom), but also BT and other telecommunications companies are expanding their range of products and services. For example, they provide computer data transmission services, and some sell a range of electronic equipment, in addition to providing information for sale.

Telephones are widely distributed in homes in the Western world. Consumers may not have noticed the wide-ranging changes to networks as microelectronic equipment has been introduced. They perhaps take for granted the improved quality of the lines and the widespread availability of national and international self-dialling. What they are more likely to notice are the push-button dials and the 'intelligent' receivers. For instance, telephone numbers can be stored and recalled for automatic redialling. Other innovations include the cordless telephone, improved switchboards and extensions, plug-in handsets, etc. Telephones can be installed in private vehicles and are frequently available for public use on long-distance trains. A very recent development is the possibility for the receiver to record the telephone number of the caller. This possibility may cut down the instances of abusive calls, but it has some privacy implications.

None of this, by itself, improves the supply of information to the home. However, by making the telephone more available and its use easier, the potential to retrieve information is improved. The telephone is an important tool for the supply of personal information because our most important sources of information are other human beings. When asked a specific question, the right person can supply a quick and accurate answer. The telephone is an important tool for helping to locate and communicate with the right person. The telephone directory, including the 'Yellow Pages' section, is an essential tool in this respect.

A comparatively recent development is the recorded information services which make available spoken information on specific topics. The user chooses the correct number to dial from a directory and connects to the recorded service. An example is the 0898 service in the UK. Numbers prefixed by this code correspond, for example, to recorded information services, or can be used to collect opinions, or conduct telephone polls. The charge is usually a flat rate which is added to the subscriber's bill. A proportion of the fee is transferred by the telecommunications company to the information service provider. Examples of services include medical information and share prices, as well as some more dubious topics! The success of these services is probably due to a combination of their ease of use, low price and predictable cost, immediate availability and ease of billing and, of course, the fulfilment of an information need.

The normal telephone handset has a limited number of functions. However, when used to connect a computer terminal, or a personal computer, to the telephone network, it becomes possible to use computer-based information services. An example in the USA is the 'Compuserve' information service. The use of this, and other on-line services, is discussed below in the section on the personal computer. Minitel, the French videotext service, also deserves a mention at this point. The idea behind this successful service from the French PTT was to automate the telephone directory by putting a very simple, inexpensive terminal in the home. However, it was realised that the terminal could also be used to provide access to a range of information and other services, such as theatre bookings and teleshopping. At least one French bank, BNP, offers a home banking service through Minitel. Using a standard terminal, it is possible to obtain details of accounts, transfer funds and order new cheque books. Minitel also serves as a device for electronic mail. An important reason for Minitel's success has been the extremely low price of the terminal, combined with the ability to bill value-added services through the subscriber's bill. In addition there was, from the outset, a well-defined first-use (the on-line telephone directory) to stimulate the use of the network. In fact, the French service was not the first to appear, but it is by far the most successful. According to the Commission of the European Communities, France has around nine out of ten videotex terminals, numbering some 5.2 million.[5]

In contrast to the Minitel system, the development of videotex services, such as Prestel in the UK, never realised the hopes of the developers. Instead of penetrating the mass market, videotex services are used in niche markets, such as travel agents, for specific tasks, such as the booking of package holidays. Around 155,000 terminals are in use in the UK.

The future offers some startling developments in communications networks. We are told that ISDN (Integrated Systems

Digital Networks) are just around the corner, or even available in some countries. They will provide data, voice and
picture transmission over the same lines. Whether they will be
inexpensive enough to appeal to the home user remains to be
seen. If they are, they will no doubt provide new possibilities
for information provision to the home.


## Personal computers

### Use in the home

The personal computer (PC) influences all sections of Western
society. Its development over the last fifteen years or so, has
been remarkable. Ten years ago, machines for the home could
be used to program in Basic, play games and little besides.
Many homes now have machines with features not dissimilar
to those used in businesses. A typical system will comprise an
8 or 16-bit central processor, a colour monitor with a graphical
display and diskette drives. Fixed discs, commonly called
hard or winchester discs, are also commonplace. Home machines will often run the wide range of software commonly seen
in businesses.

Typically, the prices of personal computers, aimed at the
home market, benefit from a mass market, although the
machines do not appear in as wide a range of homes as the
telephone. The widespread use of personal computers in home
businesses also increases the number available for other
purposes in the home. Around £500 is probably a typical price
for a home computer, or around double that amount for a
machine for a home business in the UK.

The market for home computers has not been as big as some
companies would have liked. One source[6] predicted, however,
that 24 per cent of US households would have a computer at
home by the end of 1989 and that the figure will rise to 31 per
cent by the end of 1992. IBM failed with its first home
computer, but the company sees an important market with the
introduction of its second machine.[7] The potential to supply
PCs to home businesses is clearly there in the UK as well as
the USA. A recent survey[8] by British Telecom indicated that
over 21 per cent of its customers are 'working or running a
business at home'.

One aspect of the use of the PC in the home is the very real benefit that they bring to handicapped persons.[9] Speech synthesis and recognition equipment can be connected, and the content of a display can be read with a special braille attachment. Unfortunately, some of the equipment is very expensive.

Online information retrieval systems are used in the home. Those services aimed at libraries are expensive for home use, but cut-price services have been introduced, notably in the USA. One example reported by Gutis[10] is the use in the home of the American Airlines reservation system (Eaasy Sabre). The system is, apparently, not frequently used to book a seat from home. However, it is often used as a source of information on fare and travel schedules, details of hotels, car rentals, etc.

Bulletin boards are also widely available. *Byte*, a computer magazine, has an online information service ('Bix') which provides online full-text articles, electronic mail and can download programs. It is possible to have correspondence with writers in the magazine, as well as with other subscribers. The annual cost is a flat rate of $156 plus the telecommunications charge.

## Hardware factors

It is necessary to have a mechanism for storing information permanently on a personal computer and a fast method of retrieving it. Magnetic discs are the main medium used. Most home computers have diskette drives and many have fixed discs as well. However, even these are limited in the amount of information they can store. Large capacity discs are available, but they are normally seen on more powerful business machines.

Of all the personal computer peripherals, those based on optical technology have the potential to alter radically the supply of personal information. This is partly due to their large capacity. The widespread use of the compact disc in hi-fi reproduction equipment is probably the most important factor at present. It has been shown that technology must be available at the right price for it to appeal to the mass market. The CD has radically changed the hi-fi market: its PC variant, the CD-ROM, may well, in the future, improve the supply of PC-based information in the home.

Lasers have been used to store and retrieve data since the 1970s. Video discs are used to store moving and still images, textual data and sound. However, they did not become the mass market that the manufacturers hoped they would. They were looked on as competitors to the video recorder, the latter having the overwhelming advantage that television programmes could be recorded by the user as required.

Optical discs broadly fall into three categories:

1. discs which have the date encoded in the surface at the factory and cannot subsequently be altered: CD-ROMs and video discs fall into this category;
2. discs which have the unfortunate title 'WORM' (Write-Once-Read-Many times): they can be written to as required, but once only in a particular place on the disc;
3. erasable discs to which data can be written more than once.

To be successful in the home, services and equipment have to compete with other purchases coming from the home budget. Equipment for the home is in a mass market and, hence, prices benefit from volume production. The compact disc (CD) audio has been successful in this market because, in addition to the technological advantages and standardisation, the price has been low enough to compete with other media. There are several versions of the CD which vary in the type of data stored, in the way data are placed on them and their subsequent use. Up to now, only one, apart from the audio CD, has had some success, albeit limited. This is the CD-ROM.

The CD-ROM (Compact disc read-only memory) has been fairly widely adopted in limited numbers in the information industry. At present, CD-ROM is of little interest to home users. This is partly due to the price of the equipment and partly to the lack of availability of interesting material. According to the company Info Tech,[11] there were 177,000 CD-ROM drives installed by 1989. There could, however, be a large increase in the use of CD-ROMs with the reduction in the price of portable computers (laptops), the increasing quality of flat screens and the inclusion of CD-ROMs as standard, or as built-in options, in some machines. Whilst it is unlikely in the foreseeable future that the latest best seller will be put on CD-ROM, it is realistic to expect that reference works, encyclopaedias, poetry and classics and similar items will find their way onto this medium. Indeed, a CD containing the works of Shakespeare has just been introduced in the USA at a cost of $159. The CD-ROM has a capacity of around 500 megabytes of data, which is enough to store a couple of hundred thousand pages of text on a single disc. Sony is reported to be developing a portable computer to be called 'Data-Discman', which will be like an electronic book, weighing under a kilogram. It will have a three-inch CD-ROM and hold 100,000 pages.

CD-ROM has had some success in the business and professional markets: CD-I (Compact Disc-Interactive) is aimed at the larger home market. It stores text, still and movie pictures and sound. Although still in the early stages of development, the intention is to provide an integrated electronics system which will provide audio, vision and computer power in the home. It is possible that this, or similar, equipment will be commonplace in homes by the end of the century, providing interactive games and education as well as normal TV and hi-fi sound. Interactive language learning is a frequently quoted possible application. CD-I players are not yet in the home buyer's market, and it may well be that businesses will be the first customers. Other variants of the CD include CD-ROM XA (a subset of CD-I) and DVI (Digital Video Interactive) which, by a clever compression system, stores reasonably long video sequences on the CD.

Whichever multimedia system wins out, this approach is surely going to have a big impact on home electronics. IBM, itself, admits it is an important area. James Cannavino, President of IBM's Entry Systems Division, is quoted as saying 'multimedia is no longer a tomorrow's dream, its time is now and IBM intends to be the leader'.[12] Despite what the manufacturers say, we are not there yet, and one must be sceptical about short-term dreams.

There seems little likelihood of the WORM and erasable optical drives coming to the home market in the near future, although, of course, they can easily be added to many microcomputers which appear in the home. Given, however, that they are increasingly likely to be used by small businesses, and that a large number of these businesses are run from home, their appearance in some homes can be foreseen. The

impact on personal information provision is not likely to be as
great as the CD, as the latter are more properly regarded as a
publishing/information supply medium.

### Software factors

Software is the essential ingredient which makes a computer
useful, interesting, fun or perhaps all three simultaneously.
Broadly speaking, there are two types. The first is the operating system and related tools, such as compilers and database
managers. The second are the application programs themselves. It is sometimes difficult to fit some programs into these
two categories. For instance, a database manager can be
either a tool for a programmer, or an application program
when used to store data directly. It depends to some extent on
how they are used. The operating system is like the general
manager of the office. Usually, different computers use a
different operating system. However, many manufacturers
have adopted the model used by IBM for its personal
computers. The around 40 million 'IBM compatible' PCs
mostly use the Microsoft DOS operating system. There are
some programs which have been developed with the home
worker specifically in mind. An example is 'PcRemote', which
allows the user at home to connect a PC at home to the office
computer and use the latter exactly as if he, or she, were at
work.[13]

Manufacturers other than IBM, such as Apple, Commodore
and Atari, have had success in the home market despite
having their own operating systems, or using systems different from MS-DOS. They have achieved this by offering some
particular advantage to the home user. This might be more
and better games programs, good graphical displays, low
prices, ease of use, or a combination of these and other factors.

Although this is not the place to describe operating systems
for PCs (there are plenty of computer books on that subject),
one development does deserve a mention — the graphical user
interface (GUI), sometimes known as WIMP (Windows, Icons,
Mouse and Pointer). The GUI provides a more friendly user
interface through the use of a graphical display with windows, pointing device (mouse) and icons. (An icon is an image
which represents a common object, e.g. a filing cabinet.) They
have revolutionised the interaction with computers and most

PC computer operating systems now offer this approach, which is easier for ordinary non-computer specialists to use. Instructions are given in a graphical way, and the approach is very intuitive and easily learnt. This is important for home use, when the amount of expertise is likely to be low (apart from real enthusiasts!). The influential US *PC Magazine* believes 'it is going to be a graphical interface world'.[14]

The origins of the GUI lie back in the 1970s, but it was Apple Computer which brought the technique to the personal computer world in the early part of the last decade. Microsoft added a graphical approach to DOS with the 'Windows' system. The windows allow the PC user to see information displayed from different programs. For instance, it is possible to have two documents displayed on the screen simultaneously. The programs which use the window displays can also employ a range of techniques to help the user control the program. For instance, the user employs a mouse to control a screen pointer in order to select items from drop-down menus and can 'push radio buttons'. The latter are selectable items in a menu where only one can be chosen. This is analogous to selecting the long, medium or short wave on a radio, hence the name.

The GUI represented an important precondition for the development of hypertext systems. Not only does hypertext allow data to be organised in a structured manner, but the systems also allow data to be displayed in this manner and searched by 'wandering' through them. Data can be text, diagrams, animated sequences, pictures, video and sound. An example of a hypertext system is the Glasgow Online system, described in a previous chapter.

Multimedia information systems, involving new generations of personal computer and consumer electronics equipment together with multimedia software, have an enormous potential in the home market. Graphical user interfaces and hypertext-like approaches will be essential parts of these developments. Most of the software and databases will entertain, rather than inform the user. However, systems to inform, educate and train in the home will be available, perhaps because the equipment will be bought in the first place by the mass market for entertainment purposes.

Back to the present day, where it is noticeable that the use of the personal computer in the home involves similar software to that used at work. The popular packages are the standard word-processing, database and spreadsheet applications. The purchase of software for the home puts the user in a quandary. The acquisition of the packages from the leading manufacturers can easily lead to outlays greater than the cost of the machine itself. The alternatives employed to get around this problem include using unauthorised copies, or purchasing alternative software from cheaper sources, such as those in the 'public domain'. Computer bulletin boards are one source of such software, and it can be 'downloaded', i.e. transferred from the central computer to the PC through the telephone network.

The major software suppliers have tended to ignore or miss this potentially huge market. Some, however, have introduced software packages which include fewer features than equivalent products for the business market. They are thus designed for the home market and sold at a much lower price than the prevailing prices for software used at the office. An example is Microsoft 'Works', an integrated program with spreadsheet, word processor, database and communication modules. IBM is shipping this package with its new home machine. Software is available to support a range of tasks in the home, such as helping to complete tax returns, designing a house,[15] painting and drawing programs.

Whatever software prices prevail in the United Kingdom, some purchasers look with envy at the low prices prevailing in the United States for almost identical products. Prices for non-English versions in other European countries are usually even greater than UK prices. It therefore remains a challenge to the software companies to produce a range of home software with consistent and easy-to-use interfaces for prices that the user will pay.

## Magnetic stripe and 'smart' cards

We are under pressure to hold an ever-growing collection of credit cards issued by banks, credit companies and stores. They are invariably of the magnetic stripe variety, although the so-called 'smart' cards are beginning to appear. The latter are, so far, more popular in France than in the UK.

A magnetic striped card has a standard size and contains a

memory of several hundred bytes. This is enough to store some basic data for applications, such as:

1. credit cards (personal information numbers (PIN) and card number);
2. telephone cards (amount of credit);
3. security access cards (security code, name, etc.).

Smart cards have a small chip embedded in the surface of the card, which provides a larger memory than the magnetic type, in addition to a small processor. The memory is made from EPROM (erasable programmable read-only memory), or EEPROM (electrically erasable programmable read-only memory). Both these types of memory can be reused with varying degrees of difficulty, which means that the card can be recharged with new data. Capacities of up to sixty-four kilo bytes are available at present. In addition to the smaller memory, magnetic striped cards have several disadvantages from the point of view of the organisation issuing them, compared with smart cards. The chip in the smart card provides an area of memory that is relatively tamper-proof.

Potential and existing applications of the smart card include:

1. hospital and medical records (a patient carries around his, or her, record and personal details for payments into a private scheme and in case of accident);
2. pay television (cards can be encoded with credit and with a key to decode encrypted television);
3. cash cards (a card can be 'filled' with an amount of cash which can then be deducted from the card in the shops, etc.).

Smart cards have not yet been as successful as magnetic striped cards. There are different designs of chip available, and, until a preferred design emerges, the major banks are likely to be reluctant to support them. They are also expensive relative to magnetic cards.

A variant of the smart card is the optical card, on which several megabytes of data can be stored. High cost and lack of standardisation are also amongst the reasons for the lack of usage of the optical cards. Optical storage is still a young technology, however.

## Home information systems

Although not widely available, there are systems available which will assist with home management. An obvious example of this is home security. Sensors can be attached to doors and windows. Detectors can be used to detect movement, heat, etc., and the whole series of detectors can be connected to a piece of electronic equipment which can automatically make an alert call if there is an intruder.

Less sinister uses could be the remote control of heating equipment, or cooking equipment. How luxurious to be able to have a casserole cooked when one arrives home without setting the cooker until one actually leaves the office. These systems are already in use, but not for most of us. They are clearly only for those who already have all the essential equipment, perhaps several times over.

The United States Electronic Industries Association is developing what it calls the Consumer Electronic Bus (CEBus). The intention is to standardise the control of electronic equipment in the home.[16] An article on the SUPERCOMM 90 conference[17] describes a seven-room demonstration home, complete with high definition television with digital surround sound, voice mail, homework assistance over the ISDN, home shopping, home medical monitoring, energy management and security. Will this be the home of the future?

## References

1. *The New York Times* 29 March (1990), **139**, p. B1.
2. S. K. Yoder (1990) 'HDTV, DAT technologies fall victim to US politics at electronics show', *The Wall Street Journal*, 9 Jan. p. B7.
3. K. A. Frenkel (1989) 'HDTV and the computer industry', *Comm. ACM.*, **32**(11), Nov. pp. 1300–13.
4. G. Gilder (1990) 'Television is dead', *PC-Computing*, **3**(2), February, pp. 84–9.
5. *I'M Information Market* (1990) no. 62, May–June, p. 5.
6. M. Henricks (1989) 'PCs aimed at the office create mass-market appeal', *PC World*, **7**(6), June, pp. 53–4.
7. L. Hooper (1990) 'Low-priced IBM home computer to be launched in the early summer', *The Wall Street Journal*, 25 April, p. B4.
8. British Telecom Marketing letter June 1990.

9. H. Brody (1989) 'The great equaliser — PCs empower the disabled' *PC-Computing,* **7**(2), p. 82.

10. P. S. Gutis (1989) 'More trips start at a home computer', *The New York Times,* **139**, 23 Dec., p. 23(N), 54(L).

11. L. Press (1989) 'Thoughts and observations at the Microsoft CD-ROM conference' *Comm. ACM,* **32**(7), July, p. 784.

12. J. Corfino and Steven Burk (1989) 'Multimedia stirs a revolution in corporate U.S.', *PC Week,* **6**(35), 4 Sept., p. 169.

13. T. Lahman (1990) 'Utilities: PcRemote lets you work at the office without leaving home', *PC Magazine,* **9**(1), 16 Jan., p. 287.

14. J. Seymour (1989) 'The GUI: an interface you won't outgrow', *PC Magazine,* **8**(15), 12 Sept., p. 97.

15. *Mac User* (1990) 'Designing your own home: architecture', **6**(5), May, p. 38.

16. G. Hanover (1989) 'Networking the intelligent home. The consumer electronic bus standard', *IEEE Spectrum,* **26**(10), Oct., pp. 48-9.

17. D. Bushaus (1990) 'The future will be at SUPERCOMM', *Telephony,* **218**(13), 26 March, pp. 22-3.

# Epilogue

By its nature, a big mainframe computer must be owned by a large institution — military, industrial, etc. Microcomputer power, on the contrary, is available to the population at large. Increasingly, however, the mainframes can be accessed from the micros via electronic networks. The resulting public/private interfaces will affect more and more of what the general public does. Various aspects of this interaction have been looked at in this book. What, then, are the overall conclusions?

The first point is that developments have so far been fragmentary: particular aspects of the public/private interface have been changing rapidly, but often in isolation from other aspects. Home-working provides a good example. Something like 25 million people in the United States are currently estimated as working at home on computers. Of these 9.5 million are self-employed, whilst the remainder are working at home on behalf of others. The electronic home office now represents one of the fastest-growing markets for the purchase of cheap information technology. This trend towards home-working (though not always linked to the use of new technology) is also visible in the UK. A letter recently circulated to its customers by British Telecom begins:

> Imagine not having to go into work every day. It's something I just dream about. But according to the questionnaire I have just sent you, over 20% of our customers are achieving this — by working or running a business from home.

Along with micros and communications modems, home offices are typically being equipped with printers, copiers, fax machines and so on. The indications are that these various items of equipment will soon be integrated together into workstations — single terminals from which all the information activities of the job can be handled. Yet even such workstations are not yet conceived as handling all the information requirements of an individual. For example, mass media entertainment is normally channelled via other equipment. So, though the need to think in terms of information needs, rather than technological demarcations, is now recognised, its implications are still not properly reflected in the technology available.

More generally, dedicated terminals are likely to lose some, but not all their ground to multi-purpose terminals in the future. For example, banks will continue to provide automatic teller machines for their customers to use, and the range of services offered by such machines will increase. But banks will also need to allow access to their facilities via a range of customer-owned machines, which will be used by their owners for a wide variety of other purposes.

To take the home example further, consider the range of activities envisaged for a 'wired-up' home. It is supposed that one local area network in a house will cater for radio, television, telephone, personal computing, remote shopping and banking, gas/water/electricity metering, information enquiries and so on. The important development with such a network is that it allows for interaction outside the home, as well as within it. Thus, in order to shop at a distance, the customer and the shop computer must be able both to send and receive information. From the user viewpoint, the problems are evident — the need to understand what is happening, and how to manipulate the information. But the providers also have problems. Some relate to the technology. For example, interactivity is best carried out via wideband cable connections. This offers no difficulty to a country such as the United States, where cable television is common, so that appropriate networking is in place. For a country such as the UK, where there has been greater emphasis on satellite communications, the lack of cabling currently represents an obstacle to interactivity.

Other problems relate to the information, itself. When

interaction is possible, pressures are likely to grow for it actually to occur. For example, if television viewers are in a position to comment on the programmes they watch, various groups — such as programme producers and advertisers — will be interested in the results. Hence, the system will certainly be used to carry out opinion polls. But these may have negative effects on programme content. Thus, in the USA, some attempt has been made to use such electronic polls in determining which news items shall be analysed in detail. The drawback to this is that items of minority interest rarely receive enough support in the polls to be selected for analysis. The overall effect is equivalent to saying that much of the information in 'quality' newspapers should be ignored by television.

The importance of radio and television as a guide to the technological future is clear. On the one hand, an analysis of listener/viewer requirements and reactions is probably as good an indicator as any as to what is needed for mass use of information technology. On the other, the television screen, in particular, provides a natural introduction and focus for network activities. Television is thoroughly accepted by a vast majority of the population as a means of accessing information. Yet we still tend to put information acquisition into a series of boxes. For example, news items can be acquired in various forms. One consists of up-to-date, visually-based information, which is obtained via television. Another is text-based and detailed, obtained via daily newspapers. These two types of news have been provided in the past by quite distinct organisations. The picture for the future is of integration occurring not only in the way information is output, but also in the way it is gathered and made available. Expectation of this development is already leading to change and amalgamation amongst the various kinds of organisation that handle information.

This reorganisation is being accompanied by the recognition that electronic information is essentially multi-media; that is, it can be presented equally readily in a variety of different forms, depending on the needs of the particular situation. This is the theory, at least: practice, as usual, lags a little way behind. For example, easy reading of text from television requires appreciably higher-resolution screens than are currently available. But it is, as yet, not easy to predict the extent to which new media will either supplant, or complement each other. Thus, various attempts are under way to produce an electronic 'book'. Will the products prove to be any kind of rival to the traditional printed book? One thing is evident. The old divisions between groups of users — the mass media audience, business people, schoolchildren, etc. — breaks down as information handling becomes increasingly integrated. This last point is particularly relevant for information specialists: users of all kinds will ultimately expect all their information needs to be satisfied by an integrated multimedia response.

Our interest in this book has concentrated on the problem of matching users' information wants, or needs, with the appropriate information sources. The question is how well the information needs of everyday life will be satisfied in the future, as information technology makes an increasing impact on many everyday activities. Users are typically concerned with three factors — is the system user-friendly; does it provide the range of information they require; how expensive is it? Take a television set, for example: it is easy to use, and is cheap enough for most families to afford. The advent of new television channels, especially via artificial satellites, has however, raised a query about coverage and the trade-off between this and the greater costs of accessing new channels. Compare television with a microcomputer accessing online databases. The cost of the micro may be rather more than that of a television set, but is of the same order of magnitude. The difference comes in the cost of connecting to, and searching, the databases, which is pro rata far more than the cost of a television licence. Whether the coverage provided by the databases is adequate will depend on a user's interests. Anyone interested in scientific information may be satisfied, but someone interested in novels will be less happy. Finally, few novices find accessing databases a user-friendly process. On virtually all counts, therefore, micro-based access to databases, in its present form, is hardly going to contribute to everyday information-handling. This is not to say that information retrieval by lay people is impossible: the popularity of the Télétel system in France demonstrates that this need not be true. But the factors have to be right. In the French case, this included distribution of free terminals, and a restriction to very simplified types of access.

The difficulty of accessing a database lies not only in the need for relatively complex interaction at the keyboard, but also in the formalised structure of the information itself. The public at large reacts better to information presented in a fairly informal way, since this is the style generally encountered in everyday life. The style, in turn, is related to the type of information involved. Returning to television, what it transmits might be divided into three categories — entertainment, straight information and advertising. The most appreciated of these by the audience as a whole is entertainment, which certainly represents informally structured information. It will be remembered that the initial breakthrough with microcomputers involved computer games. Yet, information technology, up to the present, has been more concerned with factual, formally structured information. The implication is that not only must the technology become more user-friendly; so must the way the information is presented and structured, a point stressed throughout this book.

Changes in the way the public accesses information will be paralleled by changes in that public, itself. The increasing number of elderly people in the population, the number of people in the work-force making mid-life career moves and the fall in the number of unskilled, as compared with skilled, workers will all affect what is acceptable both in terms of technology and of information. A detailed knowledge of the user population will be increasingly necessary in order to fit what is provided to what is needed. Above all, training, whether at school or afterwards, will be necessary to give everyone reasonable access to the new information-based activities now developing. Yet it is difficult to feel totally optimistic that the new information technology will automatically fall into place. Maybe three-quarters, or more, of the population of a developed country should be able to move sufficiently with the times that they can keep up with the new technology and the new information affecting their lives. But whether the remainder will do so is a moot point. Those disadvantaged — in terms of education, finance, family stability, etc. — may find their position in a worse state with information technology, than it has been in the past. To information specialists, interested in ways of satisfying the information needs of all the population, this last group, perhaps the least considered in information technology terms to date, may well pose the largest problems in the future.

# Index